T0077879

SPIRITUAL AMBITIONS

How Rich Do You Want to Be in Eternity?

TOM SCHULTE

WESTBOW
PRESS®
A DIVISION OF THOMAS NELSON
& ZONDERVAN

WestBow Press books may be ordered through booksellers or by contacting:

WestBow Press
A Division of Thomas Nelson & Zondervan
1663 Liberty Drive
Bloomington, IN 47403
www.westbowpress.com
1 (866) 928-1240

ISBN: 978-1-9736-1317-6 (sc)
ISBN: 978-1-9736-1319-0 (hc)
ISBN: 978-1-9736-1318-3 (e)

Library of Congress Control Number: 2018900033

Print information available on the last page.

WestBow Press rev. date: 1/3/2018

Contents

Acknowledgments

It is truly impossible for me to acknowledge everyone who contributed to this effort. Special thanks go to my longsuffering wife, who endures my many foibles, including writing. Others challenged my spiritual thinking, forcing me to dig deeper or to identify incomplete areas. Many others encouraged me to "put pen on paper" and publish. Still others helped develop the administrative part, from selecting a potential publisher to completing tax information.

1

Introduction

In 2013, I sensed God wanted me to write my spiritual ambitions. I planned on retiring soon and needed new focus. After prayer, I developed eight ambitions. My list is similar to many people's bucket list, detailing what they want to do before they die, except my list addresses my spiritual life. I will never be able to say I achieved my list of spiritual ambitions. Hebrews 2 warns us against "drifting." I decided to make these ambitions my life's priority, and not drift aimlessly from one spiritual activity to another. I can compare or test everything in my life against these ambitions.

I can't move toward these ambitions by myself, no matter how hard I try. All I can do is give God permission and put myself in positions where God can touch me. This includes what I read, think, and do. I believe God wants these ambitions for me more than I want them.

My list is as follows:

- To experience God's presence
- To be filled with God's love

- To hear the gentle wind of God
- To inspire others to obtain fruit for God's kingdom
- To have inner spiritual peace
- To have boldness to do as I hear
- To be used with power
- To see the times.

Why do I recommend people develop their own ambitions? We like to say we want to be intentional with life. I don't want to reach life's end and be any more disappointed than necessary. I don't want to add to the existing wasted time, effort, and focus in my past.

As an aside, the devil wants to steal God's mission for you. He doesn't want you to have one. He will tell you every lie from the pit, whisper in your ear, "It is too late. You have done too much, gone too far, and are too unimportant, or it doesn't matter." The devil will tell you can't, you're not cut out for it, and you can't speak or think or study like it requires. He will help you to be lazy, put it off, or whatever lie will keep you from seeing and doing God's plan or mission for you. The Bible says people perish without a vision (see Proverbs 29:18). The devil wants everyone to perish, and the sooner the better. Critical to your God-given vision is your spiritual ambitions.

Develop your own list, and then study it. What does scripture say about these ambitions, both in what they are and how to strive for them? Paul said this:

> Do you not know that those who run in a race
> all run, but one receives the prize? Run in such
> a way that you may obtain it. And everyone who

competes for the prize is temperate in all things.
Now they do it to obtain a perishable crown, but
we for an imperishable crown. Therefore I run
thus: not with uncertainty. Thus I fight: not as
one who beats the air. But I discipline my body
and bring it into subjection, lest, when I have
preached to others, I myself should become
disqualified. (1 Corinthians 9:24–27)

It is about training and discipline, not for training and discipline's sake, but to live a better Christian life. Paul said we run for an "Imperishable Crown." In 1 Corinthians 3:12, Paul writes about our eternal rewards, the gold, silver, precious stones, wood, hay, or straw. There is a clear hierarchy here. Gold is better than silver, which is better than precious stones, etc. Paul talks about judgment fire testing our works. The first three survive; the last three do not. They determine our wealth in eternity.

Interestingly, wood is more valuable than hay. You build things with wood, burn it for heat, etc. Hay is more valuable than straw. You feed hay to animals for food. The only thing straw is good for is to throw it into the animal pens to provide a dry mixture. That is, a farmer adds straw to the cattle pen. It mixes with the manure to make the animals more comfortable when they lay down to sleep. None of the six types of works are totally worthless, but only gold, silver, and precious stones make it through the judgment. We often sacrifice better things (the gold or silver) for the comfortable things (straw).

I don't want to add any more of my life to spiritual manure.
Our ambitions really determine what kind of person we

are. The kind of person we are determines what we do, which determines our eternal fruit. The eternal fruit can either be godly, which is the riches of heaven, or not, which burns up. This is a powerful reason to have the spiritual ambitions God wants us to have. Nothing else leads to gold rewards. Human works, which come from human ambitions, lead to wood, hay, and straw.

Notice what is not one of my spiritual ambitions. I am not interested in a healing ministry, a prophetic ministry, nor do I want to be a pastor, or a world-famous evangelist. I don't want the spiritual spotlight. I promise to consider suing anyone who puts my face on a billboard for any reason. I don't care what you think of me. You don't have to invite me to speak at your church, although I've spoken at several. There are many things not lining up with my ambitions, which, in and of themselves, are good things. They are just not for me, and while I might do them, I won't seek to do them. They could be, and probably are, appropriate for others.

My ambitions are progressive, building on each other. Everything starts with God's presence and then His love. People are more complex than a simple list, and while God's presence starts the system, I can work on each of these. If God is truly directing me, in one season He may emphasize boldness and later emphasize His presence. Or He may want to deal with all of them at once. Some seasons may be rest, and others may be filled with activity. He is Lord, and I gave Him myself when I made Him Lord. He determines the what and when. Submission to Jesus, not my own will, is key.

I strongly recommend everyone spend time developing their own spiritual ambitions. Don't copy mine or some preacher's, but develop your own, although you might use mine to build on and develop yours. Determine in your mind what your ambitions are, and then pursue them with everything you have. Be brutally honest. Then, look at your ambitions and compare them with what you want them to be. Maybe your ambitions need to die and be replaced by more godly ambitions. Ask God to make that switch. Bathe your list in prayer, and then start with the first one. Study it, and determine, scripturally, as much about it as you can.

Then put into place those things that make it possible for God to work your ambitions. Most likely these things include hearing God, reading the Bible, prayer, and other spiritual disciplines. How and what you do to put it into place requires insight from God. For example, if your ambition is to work with prison inmates, then volunteer at the local jail, or maybe in a soup kitchen.

Be aware that God usually asks us to do something small, then gradually moves us to bigger projects. Learn what scripture says about your ambitions, and how to express them in your daily life. Never forget to follow the Holy Spirit as you move forward. Let Him guide you in setting, researching, and following your ambitions. Don't be concerned about setbacks, as they may be stepping stones rather than delays.

Perhaps your ambitions change as you change. Life consists of seasons, and God may want to adjust your focus. Follow His guidance, and when you stand before Him at the judgment, you will hear, "Well done, My good and faithful servant." I do not believe there is a higher reward for all of eternity.

2

Setting Your Spiritual Ambitions, Part I

Every human being has mental, physical, spiritual, and emotional components. These components don't operate in a vacuum; each influences the other, and they are also influenced by things outside themselves. Saying it differently, we all influence each other, for good or bad. How many competitors say their sport is mostly mental, whether it is golf, football, or any other? The papers are full of stories of athletes overcoming emotional challenges, some unbelievably tragic. If I injure myself, my physical pain adversely affects my mental and emotional states. Similarly, our mental, emotional, and physical circumstances influence our spiritual condition.

Our challenge is to always rise above our circumstances. Few spouses want a relationship dominated by emotions. Yet we need emotional support when illness strikes. God created us to be able to conquer our mental, emotional, and physical circumstances, and He wants us to emerge victorious. When we see people who have done this, we applaud them, we comment on how strong they are, we admire them, we compare ourselves to them, and then we hope we don't have to apply what we learned.

Spiritual components are very difficult both to understand and to improve. As spiritual beings, we face many challenges. Yet we are less well equipped to deal with spiritual issues. Society does not have the same spiritual heroes as the Special Olympics. It seems so many of our religious leaders are spiritually weak, and I have difficulty looking up to them.

Scripture says our hearts are desperately wicked and that we really can't know it. Jeremiah 17:9 (NKJV) tells us, "The heart is deceitful above all things, and desperately wicked; who can know it?" This means, in effect, that we are unable to even see our spiritual condition, much less do something about it. As an aside, we can, with great effort, do something about the symptoms of our spiritual condition. Every self-improvement program works on symptoms. The next verse in Jeremiah 17 begins a dialogue (well worth studying) about how the Lord sees our spiritual condition and is very capable of doing something about it. With His help, we can see our spiritual condition, discover what our true spiritual ambitions are, and then change them if need be. His power can change our ambitions. He wants this more than we do. When He does it, it takes less effort, is more effective, and will be longer lasting than when we try on our own.

My observations prevent me from admiring religious leaders. For a while I admired a certain televangelist until I realized everything he did was all about him. He was building a monument to himself. (Monuments belong in cemeteries, not in Christianity.) Others seem to be drifting, only wanting to get by until retirement. Still others are corrupt, not realizing every penny collected in Jesus's name was bought by the very blood of God—and shouldn't be taken lightly. Then there are those who parrot the theme of the day, whether it is faith, prosperity, prophecy, healing, etc., regardless of whether it is from God. Their ambitions, correctly or not, seem to be born from something other than God. Maybe they are not convinced of God's deity and need constant reassurance.

Then there are a few that I can admire. They may even use some of the same words as the others, but there is something different about them. Their doctrine may be messed up, but I see an honest search for God's truth, to the extent they are willing to abandon long-held beliefs. All it takes is conviction from the Holy Spirit, and they change. Common characteristics are their awe of God, their love of God, and their care for God's people. Another aside: most religious leaders usually mock and reject these few.

On January 1, I always make the same physical resolution. "This is the year I will get into shape and lose forty pounds." I say these things, sincerely convinced they are physical ambitions for me. And they are valid ambitions. However, by January 21, I am less convinced—and by March, I have totally forgotten my lofty resolutions.

What are my true physical ambitions? You might say they include not being hungry, preferring the easy chair to the gym, eating my favorite ice cream, and so on. It takes honesty to admit this—brutal honesty that is hard for me to come by. Now I have a decision. Am I content with my true ambitions, or do I need to change them? They can change, albeit not easily.

I am recommending that you make a painfully honest assessment of what your spiritual ambitions really are. What do you want? The companion question is, what will you give up for them? Knowing what we give up helps us to honestly look at ourselves. We will not let anything take the place of our most prized ambitions. Above all, make sure the Lord is in your efforts, or else it becomes superficial and symptom based. And worse, you will deceive yourself into thinking you already have the ambitions you want.

For example, suppose one of your objectives is reading the Bible through each year. Now this takes time—time you might spend hitting your snooze alarm, reading the sports page, watching your favorite TV program, or surfing social media. If there is anything that will supplant reading the Bible, then reading the Bible is not really your ambition. It is more like my resolution to lose weight. Great idea, but I'm not truly committed to it unless it is my very top priority.

Your list should be the things you actually do, not what you think you should or want to do. I have talked with numerous smokers who are going to give up smoking but so far haven't. One man told me he gave up smoking twenty or thirty times a day. Smoking is more important to him than not smoking. He has more than enough information about health hazards and costs, but he chooses smoking over not smoking. This also brings up another point. Addictions—like smoking, playing video games, abusing other drugs, etc.—make the barrier even harder. I don't want to put forth the effort it takes to give it up, and I certainly want to avoid the pain generated by giving up my addiction. This makes it even more critical to look at my behavior to establish what my ambitions really are.

I believe it is nearly impossible to have more than about eight ambitions. Even eight is too many unless they relate to each other.

What might your ambitions be?

Perhaps your ambition is preaching. Preaching is an honorable ambition.

Perhaps it is translating scripture into new languages.

Maybe it is intercessory prayer.

Maybe you want to understand scriptural mysteries, to be able to explain it to people.

You may be driven (and that is what an ambition is—it is what drives us against all odds) to reach for Jesus.

You may desire to start a street ministry.

Another option might be to engage in more private worship, as opposed to assuming a leadership role in public worship.

You may be drawn to the so-called down-and-outers.

Healing and other miracles might be your thing.

Perhaps you like to encourage other workers.

Have you demonstrated serious financial or emotional giving?

Do you really want to serve others, especially those who can't do anything for you in return?

These are all positive and potentially God-given ambitions. But maybe you only want to warm the back pew.

Maybe you don't want to think about your personal sin, the price Christ paid, or His resurrection power. You could be comfortable where you are and don't want it to change.

Maybe, like me with my New Year's resolutions, the whole question is simply too much work to think about. Yeah, great concept, but for someone else.

Maybe you like the darker spiritual things. This category includes sensationalism, movies glorifying demonic themes or outright wickedness, etc. Are your addictions too important, and are they your top priority?

If you delve deeper into spirituality, you discover that all relationships between people are fundamentally spiritual. Could your thing be power trips, gossip, hate, arguments, etc.?

Are you interested in other people's opinions (that is, do you want to be known as a spiritual person)?

How about knowledge for knowledge's sake?

I only wrote about those ambitions that I choose to embrace. I have others that need to die, such as a love of knowing something others don't know, my struggle with laziness, and a need for self-promotion, friends, recognition, and so on. I am not including these things because I don't want to glorify them in the slightest.

Pray about it. Ask God to expose your current ambitions. Then, will these be the ones you want influencing your life? Can God use them to mold you into the person He wants? Do you want it? Will they lead to eternal fruit or eternal poverty?

I hope my study will encourage you. It might be a model you can use to develop your own studies, dipping primarily into what scripture says, and then letting Jesus make an aspect alive for you. More than likely, some of your ambitions will mirror mine. I hope your top priority involves your relationship to God.

I suggest you divide your ambitions into categories.

1. Your relationship to God.
2. The kind of Christian you will be.
3. How you will serve.

I believe God desires my first three almost universally for His people:

- God's presence;
- being filled with God's love; and
- sensing the gentle wind of God.

Are your ambitions what you want? Are they what God wants? Do you want what God wants? It requires brutal honesty. It is very hard. Perhaps you need to make changes. Let God direct you. I am confident He wants better for you than you want for yourself.

It will become obvious that you don't want some ambitions once you've made your list. Others might not be so obvious until you have started a scriptural study. You could decide you don't want the ambition you're studying. Don't be discouraged because you are making progress—perhaps more than most Christians.

Prayer and meditation make God's desires clear. Remember, we have three enemies: our lying flesh, the lying devil, and the lying world.

3

God's Presence

The first question is one we often take for granted: Why do we want to experience God's presence? Why do I?

The easy answer is God created us to experience His presence. The Bible implies Adam, Eve, and God walked together in the garden after Eve's creation but before they sinned. Do you wonder what they talked about? Everything was perfect, so there couldn't have been problems. Perhaps Adam asked God about eternity or what heaven was like. Perhaps they discussed the sunset or the dew or the beauty of butterflies.

Did God open Adam's eyes to see the beauty of the distant sky, those things we can only now see with powerful telescopes, and maybe things we still can't see?

Did Adam ask God whether this plant looked better next to that one, in the garden? Maybe Adam wanted to know how much water to give his tomatoes or how to peel an onion. Maybe Adam wanted to discuss what to give Eve for her birthday.

Maybe they discussed deep theological questions, such the nature of love or grace.

Did God wear clothes? Did Adam notice and asked about it? Did God have a human form, or was it a spirit form walking with Adam? What did His glory look like?

The fact is, the Bible doesn't tell us what they talked about or what God wore. These questions are rather foolish. But we do know God walked with them in the cool of the evening. On one point, scripture is unambiguous: the experience of walking with God was an incredibly intimate time.

But just saying God created us for this intimacy is like saying "we are supposed to." It doesn't satisfy me now any more than when my mom said it.

A better answer is something in me cries out for this intimacy, and it will not be silenced. The inner cry for intimacy becomes stronger and powerful the more I chase it. Increasing intimacy with God somehow satisfies me in a superhuman way. When I move toward it, something inside me knows I am on the right track. The Bible says unless the Holy Spirit draws us, we won't come, confirming this cry is from the Holy Spirit.

There has always been this cry, but lately it has become deafening. There is an urgency I have not experienced before. Satisfying this cry requires deliberate steps.

In many ways, my spiritual life up to now has been rather aimless. I tried to do what God wants as I go about my daily life. Yet Paul said in 1 Corinthians 9:24 (NKJV), "Do you not know that those who run in a race all run, but one receives the prize? Run in such a way that you may obtain *it*."

Run in such a way that you might obtain it. I have trained for a two-day, 150-mile bicycle ride. My training allowed me to finish. Paul, by comparing our spiritual life to a race, is telling us to train, and not to train for training's sake, but to train wisely.

There are basics to any training, no matter what the sport. You work on strength, endurance, aerobic, and specific skills. It is the same with spiritual training. For God's presence, the basics are as follows:

- Confess to God that you both sin and are a sinner.
- Believe Jesus, as God, came to earth, became a man, and died to pay for your sin.
- Believe Jesus rose from the grave.
- Turn from sin, making Jesus Lord.
- Then look to the Holy Spirit to guide you.

This is simple and basic stuff. Thousands of Christians have done this and nothing more. Stopping at this point is like running a hurdle race and stopping after the first one.

The next layer is learning about God. We learn through things like worship, reading scripture, prayer, talking about God with other believers, telling others about Jesus, and obedience to the basics. We often have problems with this obedience thing.

Worship is critical. It is giving God's presence your undivided attention. Worship is another word for attention. It is what you give of yourself. You can give attention in a superfluous manner, or it can be a deeper part of you, including your emotions, mind, spirit, and soul. The more you give of yourself, the deeper your worship. Jesus said the first commandment is love the Lord your God with all your heart, mind, and soul. The operative word here is *all*. Sensual feelings have nothing to do with worship. I may not like the songs, the music, or whatever. Nothing else matters if I can give my deepest self to God. It is amazingly special that we can worship anywhere, anytime, and in fact, we should.

One can read scripture with the attitude of looking for something to prove yourself right, making yourself look good, finding a loophole for what you want to do anyway, or revealing God only. I'm changed as God is revealed.

Prayer is talking to God. Many people talk to what they hope is God, but they are not sure. Perhaps others use a prayer they memorized as a child. But conversations must be two-way streets. We must know God is listening. How might He answer? He could give direction, tell us no, or tell us we ask the wrong question, or perhaps, as He often did in scripture, ignore our part of the discussion and change the subject to what interests Him. He might put His hand on our shoulder and let us know He cares about us, which is not to say He will change our circumstance, but rather He will be with us. However, no matter which of the thousands of ways God responds, somehow prayer has Him as part of the discussion.

Talking about God to other believers is, very simply, a version of talking to God. I get tremendous joy when I hear something God has done for or with someone. Sometimes I like sharing scripture with special meaning to me or perhaps an answered prayer. What gives me joy is sharing God and the things of God. It is less important whether I share or the other person shares; I still get joy. This is not true if the other guy is being religious, trying to impress me.

Telling others about Jesus is related. It is simply explaining the basics. I love to talk about what Jesus did on the cross for me. I think I always learn something new to apply to myself. What joy! Jesus said if we confess Him before men, He will confess us before His Father. I believe some of what I sense is a down payment on the confession of Jesus to the Father.

Then there is the obedience part. We don't need additional guidance to do so many things in scripture. We know we should not lie, be stingy with money, rip off widows (or anyone else), steal, etc. Each one of us might have a different list of what we already know God wants us to do, and we can find scriptures on these and other subjects.

And then the Holy Spirit directs us to do special things. For example, I know a man we'll call Mike. God directed Mike to confess a murder from years before he became a believer, and he spent three years in prison. God told me to apologize to a professional enemy once. We should act quickly when God asks us to do things.

There is an important point about obedience often missed. To count, obedience requires selfless love. If not done in love, it becomes a contract, a legal agreement. Our hearts become cold and hard, and we often fall into bitterness. We might start resenting the less obedient and start puffing ourselves up. Our spiritual sickness adds more and more rules. We'll see the other's sin but not our own. Pride and haughtiness destroy the ambition we are striving for. We become like the Pharisees, more interested in our rules than the Ruler. God's presence becomes distant and our hearts cold. When this happens, we need to ask Jesus for His forgiveness.

All the things in this layer (worship, reading scripture, prayer, talking about God with other believers, telling others about Jesus, obedience to the basics) help drive us toward God, to sense God's presence more.

But these are only the beginning. In Isaiah 6, Isaiah saw God in the throne room. He was already a prophet, used by God. But now, he had a special experience with God.

> So I said: "Woe *is* me, for I am undone! Because I *am* a man of unclean lips, And I dwell in the midst of a people of unclean lips; For my eyes have seen the King, The LORD of hosts." (Isaiah 6:5 NKJV)

Isaiah become a prophet, seeing God's plan more clearly than most.

Moses was another prophet that had a special intimacy with God, as shown in, Exodus 33:11 (NKJV), "So the LORD spoke to Moses face to face, as a man speaks to his friend."

The two disciples, after talking with Jesus on the road to Emmaus after the resurrection, had a special time with Jesus, recorded in Luke 24:32 (NKJV), "And they said to one another, 'Did not our heart burn within us while He talked with us on the road, and while He opened the Scriptures to us?'"

When I first believed, I sensed the Holy Spirit enter my life. As time went on, I grew, and my relationship with Him changed. I learned I could not manipulate God, and He has standards. I learned I had to deal with my sin. The relationship matured. But now I look for a deeper relationship.

I have learned God wants to talk with me. It sounds silly, but it is true. He wants to have a conversation with me. This is incredibly hard. You must deal with what He says once God starts talking. You can ignore Him, which effectively tells Him to shut up, or you can pay attention. Usually what God says is worth listening to. Actually, it always is worth listening to, and more than listening, but also letting him change us or doing what he wants, and the operative word is *immediately*.

What does God want to talk about? He wants to talk about what is on His mind and what is on my mind. This is the same as two good friends; they talk about what is on their minds. Most conversations don't lead to earth-shattering change, but they are all about building a relationship. You can't have a good friend if you don't talk with him. It's the same with God. God wants me to tell Him about my day, not whining and sniveling about something, but like you might talk with your best friend. One day I had a long, pointless, mandatory meeting with my boss before starting useful work. His meeting aggravated me because at that time, I had to work nights and weekends. It is hard to believe Jesus is interested in my day at work, but He is. More importantly, He is interested in me telling Him about it, since He already knows more about it than I do.

Then there are the things in the way of my relationship. They may be bad things, like basic sin, or even good things that happen to be in the way. I have an active imagination. With this I can solve difficult problems—which is good. But my imagination allows me to think bad thoughts. These thoughts could be harmless, like imagining I am a star quarterback, or harmful, like imagining what I will do to someone who did me harm.

Anything taking time could be in the way. God told my friend Charlie to stop studying the Bible for a while and do something else. Most of us have the opposite problem, but

Charlie studied for up to ten hours per day! In his case, God was interested in balance.

You can put anything in front of God. The Bible will call anything taking His place an idol.

Marriage is similar. You must give your spouse time. Anything in the way of giving your wife your attention is a problem. If I am reading and my wife says something, I will stop reading, put down my newspaper, and pay attention to her. She may be asking me what I am reading. She has all my attention when we talk. It is critical to our relationship. I wish I were perfect in giving her attention.

There are distractions. Sometimes I'm distracted when my wife speaks. I may be thinking of a personal issue at work, or about money, or maybe a tooth hurts. Whatever the distraction, it limits closeness. It is the same way with God. All kinds of things distract us, and they all limit intimacy.

I want to sense God's presence as I go about my daily tasks. I want to actively know God is with me when I read the mail, make my lunch, walk the dog, or change my oil.

I want to talk with Him when I drive, when I exercise, and as I fall asleep. Now when I drive, I can't give Him my full attention. He understands the restriction, but we can still build our relationship. I would rather give God my attention than mindless talk radio.

But I don't want to sense Him far off. I want to sense Him close. I want to sense Him so close to me, it is like we are one. I think Jesus wants this closeness as well.

> I in them, and You in Me; that they may be made
> perfect in one, and that the world may know that

You have sent Me, and have loved them as You
have loved Me. (John 17:23 NKJV)

Our model for "one-ness" is the unity the Father and Jesus
have. It is so close the Bible says, "Hear o Israel, the Lord thy
God is One" (Deuteronomy 6:4 NKJV). Jesus prayed for unity
between believers immediately before going to the cross, and
indeed, this is an important reason He went to the cross.

So what is standing in my way? It is basic rebellion. I want
to do my thing. I want to be important, highly thought of, and
rich. I want God to accept my human works, despite knowing
what I do apart from Him is worthless. I want to be loved and
not love in return. I am selfish. I want my way. I want many
possessions, more than I can use. I want power over people.
I want to be handsome, athletic, smart, and famous. In short,
I'm a mess.

When you look objectively, you conclude so much of my
humanity needs to die. This is not saying my personality will
go, only a bunch of the things driving me or making me tick.
I really don't like dying. The other side is great, but the act
of dying is painful, and I am a coward. Giving up a desire is
similarly painful.

But God looks at me without dwelling on my mess. He
wants to gather me in His arms, hold me tight, and love on
me. He wants to comfort me, wipe the dirt off, clean me up,
and make me His.

God wants me to know His presence more intimately and
more often than I do. Why He is this way is a big mystery.

So, what am I going to do?

I am struggling to draw near to Him and to give Him

permission to let me experience Him. Once I had a long conversation with God. We talked back and forth about some of my fears and worries and what I thought were my needs and wants. I don't remember ever having that experience before. But it was hard because I had to become vulnerable.

I am getting rid of things in the way between God and me. Years ago, my wife did not like my Porsche, and while she never said a word, I got rid of it. One reason was because I didn't want it coming between us. I am thinking and praying about what is between God and me so I can get it out of my life.

I work on forgiveness. It is amazing what I must forgive.

I have sin between God and me, as I mentioned. God does not care much if I am sorry for my sin but if only I turn from it.

I am going to spend time with Him.

I am going to continue to struggle. But I am doing something else as well. Perhaps the most important, I am asking God to put in me what it takes to respond to the Holy Spirit drawing me. The struggle is bigger than me, but it is not bigger than God. He is waiting for permission.

So now, I ask you. Will you struggle with me? Do you want to know the presence of God in the most intimate possible form? Will you join me in giving God permission?

4

Filled with God's love

My spiritual ambitions are as follows:

- To feel God's presence
- To be filled with God's love
- To hear the gentle wind of God
- To inspire others to obtain fruit for God's kingdom
- To have inner spiritual peace
- To have boldness to do as I hear
- To be used with power
- To see the times

The previous chapter dealt with the foundation, which is God's presence. The next ambition is to be filled with God's love.

Love is a funny thing. We misunderstand love. Part of the problem is we rarely see scriptural love. Most of us grew up in families with at least a few problems. Our parents were human, which is another way to say they were at least occasionally selfish. We don't have a word in the English language for this special love, so we borrow a Greek word, *agape*.

Agape love is the kind of love God has for us, a selfless love. It's not shallow but totally deep. Other meanings of love, like "I love ice cream" or the sexual love between spouses or the friendship love, are lesser types. We are only discussing the agape love, shortened here to love.

We all want love. I have never talked to anyone who did not want love. We want someone to love us because of ourselves, not because of what they can get. Most women want to be loved because of themselves, not their bodies. At the deepest level, we want to be loved by someone who still loves us after clearly seeing all our faults and insecurities. This is hard, because we don't want these things to surface. We keep them hidden because we know how hard it is to love someone with such things.

And while we want love, we don't want to give love. We want the objects of our love to be perfect, or at least to do, act, and look like we want. We want our cake and to eat it too. We want the selfless love but are not willing, or perhaps not able, to love selflessly back.

Most people see and have accepted this hypocrisy. Several years ago, a guy told me he and his wife endure each other. Another person talked about how many couples did not like each other enough to do the same things on their vacations. I am lucky, because I want to do what my wife wants, and she wants to do what I want.

After a couple of years, the game gets old, and people either drop out of their marriage mentally and emotionally or get a divorce.

Several years ago, I owned a Labrador retriever named Reggie, who was one of the most neurotic dogs on the planet. But he really loved us. I feel sorry for anyone Reggie thought threatened his family, including the postman and backyard squirrels. He would give his life for his family. He followed us around the house, needing to be close to us. He was always listening, hoping to understand something we might say. Rubbing behind his ears was the closest thing to doggie nirvana he could get. Reggie was a good example of love.

> If we are going to talk about love, we need to know what it is. Apparently, this has been a question for almost two thousand years. Paul, in 1 Corinthians 13:1–13 (NKJV) tells us: Though I speak with the tongues of men and of angels, but have not love, I have become sounding brass or a clanging cymbal. And though I have *the gift of* prophecy, and understand all mysteries and all knowledge, and though I have all faith, so that I could remove mountains, but have not love, I am nothing. And though I bestow all my goods to feed *the poor,* and though I give my body to be burned, but have not love, it profits me nothing. Love suffers long *and* is kind; love does not envy; love does not parade itself, is not puffed up; does not behave rudely, does not seek its own, is not provoked, thinks no evil; does not rejoice in iniquity, but rejoices in the truth; bears all things, believes all things, hopes all things, endures all things. Love never fails. But whether

there are prophecies, they will fail; whether *there are* tongues, they will cease; whether *there is* knowledge, it will vanish away. For we know in part and we prophesy in part. But when that which is perfect has come, then that which is in part will be done away. When I was a child, I spoke as a child, I understood as a child, I thought as a child; but when I became a man, I put away childish things. For now we see in a mirror, dimly, but then face to face. Now I know in part, but then I shall know just as I also am known. And now abide faith, hope, love, these three; but the greatest of these *is* love.

Let us look a little more at these few key concepts. Love suffers long. How long will I put up with an annoyance? Biblical love says a long time. How long is a long time? Perhaps a lifetime?

Love is kind. We all know people who make jokes at their spouse's expense. Embarrassing your spouse is not kind. We know what kind is. It is doing nice things for people. It is an act of kindness to be pleasant, even when the other person is not.

Love does not envy. Can I say I am not at least a little bit jealous when my wife gets a raise or an accolade?

Love does not parade itself. I like people to know how great or smart I am. This desire is parading myself.

Love is not puffed up. I'm puffed up with pride. If I had more pride, I would have burst.

Love does not behave rudely. The world is full of rude people, most of them driving in my lane.

Love does not seek its own. In other words, love looks out for the other's best interest, even when it costs.

Love is not provoked. Stirring the pot, so to speak, is usually not love.

Love does not think evil. How many times have I seen or heard something, and immediately my mind thinks of the worst possible scenario? I once heard of a company's employee who damaged an expensive specialty truck. Although the damage was cosmetic, they sold it for almost nothing. I wanted to know who bought it—or in other words, who stole it.

Paul says worse. He says, "Love does not rejoice in iniquity, but rejoices in truth; bears all things, believes all things, hopes all things, endures all things. Love never fails" (1 Corinthians 13:6-7)

We could talk about these, but we get the picture. Love is hard.

The question that has bothered people for centuries is, "Who must I love?" Jesus said we are to first love God with all our hearts, minds, and strength. Today we say, "With everything we've got." Think back to the definition of love. Do we really love God to such an extent? And if we do, do we do it with all our strength? I don't. I hold back.

Jesus said we are to love our neighbor as ourselves. Now I love myself a whole lot. It is unbelievably hard to love my neighbor as I love myself. I must even love the crazy neighbor sitting on his front porch in his underwear holding his assault rifle. Fortunately, this neighbor is fictional, at least so far.

But hardest is what Jesus said in the upper room. We are to love the brethren as Christ has loved us. Jesus gave up being God and became a man. What He did is particularly humbling. He didn't come as a rich man but the poorest of the poor. He walked on dusty roads, and the leaders mocked Him. He let them beat Him and nail Him to a cross to die a horrible death, alone, with no friends. He took every bit of our separation from God and spent time in hell for us. He did all this because He loves us. The passion Jesus has for His people cannot be understood. It is with this passion that we are to love the brethren. Trust me, I don't love you enough to take your place on a cross.

So, I don't love God, my neighbor, or my fellow believer. I fall short.

So, what is the big deal? Why does it matter?

> Revelation 2:4–6 (NKJV), speaking to the church of Ephesus, says: Nevertheless I have *this* against you, that you have left your first love. Remember therefore from where you have fallen; repent and do the first works, or else I will come to you quickly and remove your lampstand from its place—unless you repent.

Basically, Jesus told the church at Ephesus they had better return to their first love, which is the love like when they first believed.

How did they lose this love? Well, things happen. Stuff crowds out God. There is a good football game, computer game, or something else. We are invited to go fishing. Hebrews 2:1 (NKJV) states: "Therefore we must give the more earnest heed to the things we have heard, lest we drift away." We drift away.

In the parable of the sower and the soil, some seed fell among thorns, which choked the sprouting seed. Jesus explained the thorns were the cares of the world. Time and again Jesus warns us to not worry about the future but to leave the future in God's hands. I believe this is because these cares grow and choke our love for God. It takes constant weeding in the flowerbed of life for us to keep our first love and indeed, let it prosper.

But apart from God commanding us to love, why should we want to be filled with love? Love continues into eternity. My selfless love, the kind 1 Corinthians talks about, will continue into eternity. It is possible love is the only thing we take into eternity. It may be the riches, or currency, of eternity.

I was created for love. Often I hear of someone struggling with life, and someone says, "They just want to be loved." I want to be loved as well. I was made for love, and I am not complete without love. People without love either search for it or become cynical, give up, and ignore their need.

We call people who can't love "hard." Many gangs prosper because they give an illusion of love. Prostitutes give the illusion of love, as long as you pay their price.

How do we know if we love? One thing is certain. The things we give our attention to are the things we love. The amount of time I spend thinking about my bicycle is the extent I love my bicycle, or my job, or my wife. Now, God gave me these things and they are good. Some not-good things include drugs, revenge, or pity parties. Whatever we are giving our attention to is what we show our love to.

Love must be nurtured and allowed to grow, or it will

die. If we cut off our attention, our love for those things will decrease. Ignore your pet and see how much it loves you.

An alcoholic's struggle is giving up his love of the bottle. AA, for all of its good, is a start. Fundamentally, his addiction, like all addictions, stems from his love. Booze is his love.

We only have so much time. When we spend time on other things, we will have less to spend on what we consider important. We can love reading the Bible, prayer, singing hymns of praise to God, or many other good things. When we feed these loves, the love of booze or drugs decreases.

I want to make one thing clear. AA and NA talk about a higher power. I am not suggesting they are bad or in the way, but they are one tool in this struggle.

Honesty helps build love. I must be honest with God.

Love costs. I must be willing to pay the price. It might only be someone laughing at me, or it might be worse. Jesus will be there with me through it for my comfort.

To love, I must give gifts. I can build my love of God by giving offerings to God's service. This might be money, time helping someone, or something only between Him and me.

The most important thing I can do, though, is ask God for His help in loving. He wants a loving relationship with me more than I want one with Him. When I give Him permission, He does more than simply direct me. He becomes actively involved in the process. God has a lot of power. By letting Him have free reign, I am guaranteed to overcome.

Next, and maybe at the same time, is submission. I need to submit to Him. God does not share His glory with anyone. By submitting to Him, I am giving Him the glory for changing my heart from cold and stony to lively.

One of my difficulties is God is "up there somewhere." Sure, I think, I'd do all these things if He was here. God has not given us a loophole. We are to love those He gave us, such as our spouse and children. There are plenty of other surrogates to receive love as well. He said in Matthew 25:40b (NKJV), "As you did it to one of the least of these My brethren, you did it to Me."

The Bible talks about being "filled with the Spirit." Many people say speaking in tongues and being filled with the Spirit are one and the same. We are definitely commanded to be filled with the spirit, as in Ephesians 5:18 (NKJV): "And do not be drunk with wine, in which is dissipation; but be filled with the Spirit."

Other places it sounds slightly different, such as in acts. Acts 13:8–11 (NKJV):

> But Elymas the sorcerer (for so his name is translated) withstood them, seeking to turn the proconsul away from the faith. Then Saul, who also *is called* Paul, filled with the Holy Spirit, looked intently at him and said, "O full of all deceit and all fraud, *you* son of the devil, *you* enemy of all righteousness, will you not cease perverting the straight ways of the Lord? And now, indeed, the hand of the Lord *is* upon you, and you shall be blind, not seeing the sun for a time." And immediately a dark mist fell on him, and he went around seeking someone to lead him by the hand.

Right or wrong, I think being filled with the Spirit as so filled with God's Spirit, and by extension His love, that there is no room for selfishness. If this means you speak in tongues, great. If it does not, great. The bottom line is love is the only thing we take into eternity, and being filled with it is such a good thing.

I have talked about being filled with love. As I talked about it, I mentioned things I struggle with, helping me on my life's journey. Where are you in your journey? Will you join me in asking God to fill our hearts with His love? It is not for everyone. Is it for you? I have decided, despite my struggles, that it is for me.

5

To Sense the Gentle Wind of God

Previous chapters dealt with God's presence and being filled with God's love. Now, I want to address "sensing the gentle wind of God."

I usually detect a common theme every time I talk to people about spiritual things. Each person expresses it in a thousand different ways, with saying. The question boils down to "How do I get to God." Some people might say, "How do I get peace?" Others seek truth. Still others seek money, fame, or rest. All reflect a deep need inside our souls to experience God. Everything else is only a surrogate for their critical need for God. No one, including me, is satisfied with themselves, but we reach for more—no one, except those who have given up. But even those who have given up want to experience God; only they have been disappointed to the extent they no longer believe it possible.

One reason people give up is because of lies told by others

who have already given up. It demonstrates the proverb, "Misery loves company." They teach things preventing others from getting to God. I have heard this from various pulpits, on the radio, and in private conversations. Jesus commented on this when he talked about the scribes in Matthew 23:13 (NKJV), "But woe to you, scribes and Pharisees, hypocrites! For you shut up the kingdom of heaven against men; for you neither go in yourselves, nor do you allow those who are entering to go in." But we need not be deterred. We can get to God.

Once we enter the throne room of God and experience His dramatic presence, we want more. We can't stay in the throne room, since we still must live and work in the world. Besides, God has things for us to do, and we need to get busy. Therefore, God made a way for us to stay in touch. The Holy Spirit constantly moves throughout the world, and if we are sensitive, we can hear Him, like a gentle wind.

Hearing from God is an incredibly complex subject. There are many ways to hear from God. He has been known to speak in dreams and visions directly, which is similar to an audible voice, in our thoughts, and through other people, circumstances, and so on. You could make a list and find examples of each in scripture. To limit the topic to a manageable size, I'll narrow the discussion to the gentle wind of the Holy Spirit.

I want to hear God any way He wants to speak to me. But for me, the gentle wind is one of the main ways I commune with God. I think His gentle wind is one of the most important, yet the easiest to overlook.

I use the word *commune* rather than communicate for a reason. I don't understand much of what God says. Many times I only bask in His presence. Whatever it is, it is more than an intellectual exchange but rather a oneness at the deepest levels. I am sensing God in my spirit, in the place created to sense Him. This place is something in me that came alive when I got saved.

Why do I want to hear from God? One reason is for direction. I need to hear His commands to be obedient if I make Him Lord. Another is for comfort. There are times when I'm upset, because either something bad entered my life or I'm suffering disappointment. Then there is the fellowship. I want fellowship with God. I want to talk to Him about the things important to me and listen to what matters to Him. This is why I was created (see 1 John 1:3). Fellowship is different from a petition, as I am not asking for something, but more like having something on my mind and needing to visit with Him, or He has something on His mind and wants to visit with me.

I have talked to Him about work problems, health issues, social issues, and so on. One time I was silently grieving about how my church was becoming mostly women, and I was not expecting Him to answer, when this unknown lady came to me, out of the blue, and told me God heard my prayer and would answer it. I had no idea what I was praying about. I dismissed her as a nut. But years later, God reminded me of the event and had me look around in my church. There were about as many men as women. I was not asking Him to bring more men into the church; I was only upset because there were not. Yet, He counted it as prayer.

The one thing I need the most (at least from my perspective) is peace. Real peace can only come from unity with God. I believe the reason so many are so angry and frustrated, in fact why I'm frustrated, is because we don't have peace. I need peace as I go about everything I do, whether it is driving, working, or waiting to minister. I know it only found in the quiet presence of the Holy Spirit. This peace is an inner peace and is different from a smooth life. I will address this more in chapter 6.

The same Hebrew word for wind is the word for spirit and breath. We can remember this because we talk about someone getting the wind knocked out of them. Now their spirit didn't leave, but they feel like it did. It is a tiny play on words, to help us in English. But in the Hebrew, we can only know the meaning by looking at the context.

Let's look at John 3:8 (NKJV): "The wind blows where it wishes, and you hear the sound of it, but cannot tell where it comes from and where it goes. So is everyone who is born of the Spirit."

Wind in this verse is clearly talking about weather but also about the Holy Spirit. We can see and hear what the weather and wind do, and we see and hear what the Holy Spirit does, but we don't see where either comes from or goes. I used to marvel at a gust of wind coming across a field of wheat. You could see the gust bend the grain, then suddenly you felt it, and as quickly, it was gone.

I have watched dust devils, those little whirlwinds you see on freshly farmed dirt. Kids try to catch them but never can. I never understood where they came from or where they were going, especially after they lifted off the soil.

Wind can be gentle and soothing, like a quiet spring breeze, or violent and terrifying, as in a tornado or hurricane.

The Holy Spirit can be soothing, but from what I read in the Bible, I really, really don't want to see Him mad.

The wind is everywhere. My weather expert friends tell me the wind always moves at least a little—that there are air currents always mixing and moving moisture. Without moisture, life on earth would be difficult if not impossible. Water means life, and the wind brings life. The air currents remove carbon dioxide from animals and bring fresh oxygen to us. Our lives depend on the gentle wind.

I've been told a major problem in space is without fans, there are few air currents. Astronauts exhale, but their breath stays close to them. They start breathing the same air they just used. Without the fans circulating the air, the astronauts will suffocate! Without air currents, life soon dies. Without the Holy Spirit, the believers' spiritual selves suffocate and die.

The Holy Spirit is everywhere and is always moving. He brings life. I found life difficult without Him. The Holy Spirit teaches me and guides me.

> I will instruct you and teach you in the way you should go; I will guide you with My eye. Do not be like the horse *or* like the mule, *Which* have no understanding, Which must be harnessed with bit and bridle, Else they will not come near you. (Psalm 32:8–9 NKJV)

Here God tells us to allow Him to guide us with the gentlest breeze, only a glance. He doesn't want us to force Him to put a bridle in our mouths (which most farm boys know is not exactly pleasant for the horse) and be drug, kicking and screaming, into His will.

The wind can drive great ships and for many years was the major source of power for mills to grind grain, wells to pump water, and so forth. If you have any interest in being effective in the kingdom of God, you had best act like a ship and point your spiritual sail to catch the Holy Spirit. Otherwise, you are working from human strength, which is next to worthless. It is amazing how little wind it takes for a windmill to generate electricity. It is equally amazing how gently the Holy Spirit moves to do something fantastic.

And like the captain of the ship needs skill, I need skill in directing spiritual sails to catch the wind. The only way to get skill is to practice, and God wants us to practice. I tell people to do what I did when first became a Christian. I asked God which shirt to wear. Now this was an absurd decision, because I only wore white shirts at that time and had many shirts. It was an excuse to hear God. It most likely didn't much matter about the shirt, but what did matter was practicing hearing His voice.

Sometimes when He speaks to me, I hear Him as a quiet urge, sometimes as a pull, sometimes as peace. One critically important event stands out in my mind. I felt significant spiritual turmoil. I mentally explored different actions over the course of a half hour, but the spiritual pressure only increased. God wanted me to do something, and I wasn't getting it. I finally obeyed the direction He was pulling me. Immediately I felt peace. In hindsight, it was one of the better things I have done. I don't always see God's direction, but that time I did.

Now whatever city or town you enter, inquire
who in it is worthy, and stay there till you go out.
And when you go into a household, greet it. If the
household is worthy, let your peace come upon
it. But if it is not worthy, let your peace return to
you. (Matthew 10:11–13 NKJV)

In this passage, Jesus tells His disciples about how to know
where to stay on their journey. The criterion was whether peace
was present. It was important to know where to stay but much
more important to learn to hear the Holy Spirit. I think this
was one important reason God sent them out, in addition to
their actual work. Peace is one way the wind of the Holy Spirit
communicates with us.

This peace is not the absence of conflict but instead a quiet
oil, like on a stormy sea. It has a confidence associated with it,
explaining God is in control. It connects in a special spiritual
way. It is so quiet and soft that we won't hear it if we are not
listening carefully. The devil tries to shout it down, but we must
tune him out. I want to be led by peace. I want to be led by the
slightest touch from God.

I am not sure why, except to say this is why I was created,
to sense God on a continuous basis. Anything less means I
have a major need that cannot be filled.

The wind is always present, and so is the Holy Spirit. We
never know when God wants us to change what we are doing,
thinking, or feeling. The wind of the Holy Spirit is an important
way, perhaps the most important way, God uses to guide us.
This is true even if we don't recognize His touch.

It is becoming saturated with God. It allows Him to soak

through our souls. We become marinated in Him, and one marinates steak to improve the taste.

It allows us to see God in special ways. We learn to sense His emotions. We feel His joy, His sorrow, and His concern.

Proverbs talks a lot about the value of wisdom. Soaking in the Holy Spirit brings godly wisdom, and we don't know it is happening. We are changed.

Bolero, by Ravel, is a favorite classical symphony. One section has this quiet, simple passage. Every time I hear this passage, I realize right behind the quiet part is tremendous and powerful yet restrained music. Behind the small, quiet voice of God is great yet restrained power. Elijah on the mount experienced a volcano, a tornado, and an earthquake (1 Kings 19). But when Elijah heard the small, still, quiet voice of God, he covered his head. Elijah realized the small, quiet voice had more power than the volcano, tornado, or earthquake.

I have noticed those people making the most noise are usually the most wrong. We mistake loudness with life. God does not need to shout.

How do we sense this quiet wind? It is not with a human sense but our spiritual senses. When we confess our sins, believe Jesus died on the cross, paying for our sins, and Jesus is alive and decide to make Him the boss (or lord) of our lives. Then and only then does something in us become alive. We say the Holy Spirit enters our hearts. More accurately, the Holy Spirit makes alive the part of us created to connect with God but died due to our sin. With it is a new spiritual sense. There is no way to describe the spiritual sense in human terms, because there is no equivalent. But we casually toss out words like *hearing God* or *seeing His will*. What we are trying to say is we use this newfound spiritual sense to latch onto what God is telling or showing or being.

I was frustrated for several years because I could not connect with God. My spiritual senses were dull due to sin. I had taken responsibility for something that was not my business and paid for it. Once I realized what I had done and repented, my spiritual senses "woke up." I could connect to God again.

This connection is why I was created.

This connection is why every human was created. It doesn't matter where we stand in our lives, what has happened to us, or what we have done. God still desires to connect with each person.

I know people who connected in the minutes before they died. Leo was one. Leo was highly educated but fell sick. At the last minute, he connected to God and did it through prayer. As you are dying, you realize how meaningless everything you spent your life working for really is. How much better would it have been if Leo had realized it many years before and could have experienced the wind of the Holy Spirit? Leo might not have been as successful as his boss thought he was or made as much money, but instead he would have had something of far more value, which is the presence of God. As he lay dying, all his promotions, money, and even family meant nothing.

Scripture talks about this as different kinds of works. First Corinthians 3:2 talks about the works we might build on the foundation of Jesus Christ. These works are divided into gold, silver, precious stones, wood, hay, and stubble. For the record, stubble is what the farmer leaves in the field after he harvests his crops. It is worth little, only to throw into cattle pens to help dry manure. This passage talks about these works being tested by judgement fire. The gold, silver, and precious stones pass through, but the wood, hay, and stubble burn up.

I want the rest of my life to be filled with gold, not stubble. I can't do anything about all the yesterdays, but I can about today and tomorrow. The only way for my works to be golden is for me to follow the gentle wind of the Holy Spirit.

I need that wind to drive me like the sailing ship. I need it to direct my thoughts, my emotions, and my speech. I need it to be like an aurora around me. I want God to impact people simply by my presence.

Most importantly, I want to commune at the deepest levels with God. I want Him to be more than my best friend and the lover of my soul. I want Him to change me, to make me presentable to the Father.

Years ago, a line in a song from "Jesus Christ, Superstar" touched me. That line was, "I don't know how to love Him." I can love Jesus many ways. Connecting with the Holy Spirit is one of them. Loving Jesus then leads me to love the things He loves. He loves people enough to have died for us.

In 1975, I tried to decide what was worth dedicating my life to. I concluded, of all the things I could think of, only God was worth the effort. I have a need to give myself to something, and I want it to count. The only thing worth the effort is Jesus. This realization led to my asking Jesus to be my Lord. Continually sensing Him requires total commitment.

Do I have what it takes? Can I do it? The answer is clearly no. But I can ask God, and He can give me what it takes.

In case you haven't filled in the blank, the Bible clearly says anything else is sin.

Will I ever arrive? No, not likely. I ride a bicycle for recreation. I train, study, etc., trying to be better. The bottom line is I will never win a race. But I can do better than I have done up to now.

When I fail, God forgave me when Jesus died on the cross. It is never too late to start, and we have never gone too far. I deeply regret all the times I didn't sense the Holy Spirit and reacted out of my human flesh. But I can do better. I suppose this is what Christian growth is all about.

So far so good. But you should ask, "What concrete steps do I intend to take?"

The first is to shut up. When two people have a conversation, they take turns speaking and listening. It is the same with God. Since what He has to say is more valuable than what I have to say, I need to listen more than speak. It's not that He isn't interested in what I want to say, or I shouldn't tell him what is on my mind. I can't be yammering endlessly if I want to sense the Holy Spirit.

The second is humbling myself. I can't be so full of myself there is no room for the things of God. We all know people full of themselves. Usually we don't want to be around them. God is no different; He doesn't like the arrogant either. Humbling ourselves means we become a servant. We do this in front of God. Guess what—He is watching as we interact one with another. God sees when I take a "you can't do that to me" attitude to another person. Taking the "me" attitude is not being humble.

Right along with humbling ourselves is submitting or obeying Him. All of us know how to please God in a lot of ways, but we don't do them. We don't need more truth. What we need is to do the truth we already know. We need to make His ways our ways. We need to cry with Jesus in Gethsemane, "Not my will but Yours." I learned it is okay to struggle with obedience. Jesus did in Gethsemane. After His struggle, He did what He knew the Father wanted. We can struggle, but in the end, we need to obey. Just don't struggle too long.

The fourth thing is to read scripture, especially Psalms. I have learned reading Psalms does something that changes me. The Holy Spirit reaches into my heart, and I become different. But I must do more than read the words. I must get into them. I don't understand everything, but I can't let my lack of understanding get in the way. Often, I don't understand what the Holy Spirit does in my heart when I read. But it doesn't matter.

And the last thing is to love God with everything I have. If I love God, I will love the things God loves. It means I will love the people around me, and especially love other Christians. I used to wonder what godly love was. First Corinthians 13 tells us. I don't have the time to go into this in detail, but the short answer is it doesn't matter how spiritual I am. If I am not looking out for the best interests of someone, I don't love them.

Let me summarize:

1. Shut up.
2. Humble myself.
3. Obey Him.
4. Read scripture.
5. Love God with everything I have.

Saying what goes without saying is the devil is always there, trying every way possible to either confuse me or to divert me from hearing the wind of the Holy Spirit. One of his primary tools is my fleshly desires, my need for control, my love of possessions, or power, or position, or fame, or so on. It is a continual struggle. This struggle keeps refining me and my inner soul and spirit. I am continually learning and gaining wisdom and insight, particularly in how much God loves me.

On the farm, we talked about the difference between tomato plants grown outside and those grown in a greenhouse. Greenhouse plants never seemed to do as well, which we always attributed to the weather tossing outside plants around. There is something about how adversity helps to bring fruit, both in the natural world and the spiritual world. Our loving God only allows the perfect amount of adversity to maximize our fruit but not uproot us.

As I close, I want to explore a little different aspect of this. I have been talking about it from my perspective. But God is a person, with emotions, thoughts, and plans. He has a perspective as well as I do. After all, His perspective is the one I want. What does He want? Romans 12:2 tells us there are three levels of God's will: the acceptable, the good, and the perfect. God accepts a lot, is more satisfied with good, but desires the perfect. I strive to do the perfect will of God, which I can only do if I do what Jesus did, which is to only do that which the Father said. I wish I were even a little better at achieving the perfect will of God. Fortunately, Jesus paid for my shortcomings at the cross.

He wants to commune with us at a deeper level than we will ever be able to experience or understand until we get to eternity. He is like a grandparent with grandkids playing at his feet. The kids are just kids, but Grandpa is so proud of them. A baby resting in his mother's arms brings Mom so much joy. Playing at the feet of God, resting in His arms, letting Him touch us in the most intimate way possible, brings Him great joy.

God is incredibly passionate. I believe He holds back His passion because otherwise we couldn't take it. I have been in prayer and couldn't take the presence of God.

Let's pray for spiritual intimacy. Maybe this is foreign to you. Now is a good time to use your own words and ask God for this intimacy. Maybe you express it differently, which is okay if God inspires your ambition.

6

Inspire Others to Obtain Fruit for God's Kingdom

My question is, "Why bother to witness or talk about the things of God, especially since it appears most people aren't interested?" Maybe the question is, "Why doesn't it make a change in people's lives?" Why put myself through potential rejection and hassle? Almost always my attempts go nowhere. By now I have talked to thousands of people, with what feels like little effect. It seems people determine to live lives either apart from God or only marginally in the kingdom of God. I believe this trend is getting worse.

Previous chapters addressed God's presence, being filled with God's love, and sensing the gentle wind of God. These are the basics of faith. I should mention these things are like a pyramid, starting with God's presence. I can't emphasize enough how important it is to have God's presence. Everything not done by God's power is worthless.

Now, it is time to address the fourth, which is, "Inspire

others to obtain fruit for God's kingdom." This is the response to my opening question of, "Why bother?"

Just what is this fruit stuff? Fruit is rather obvious; it is what a fruit tree makes. If you have an apple tree, you get apples. Spiritual fruit is the result of a Christian life. A tree puts all its energy into making fruit. It puts down roots, grows leaves, basks in the sunlight, and uses photosynthesis only to make fruit. A farmer with a beautiful but barren apple tree will someday cut down his tree. The farmer will nurture like a child a scrawny, ugly tree that yields much fruit.

In the gospels and Acts, there are about forty-five references to fruits.

Jesus said in Matthew 7:17 (NKJV), "Even so, every good tree bears good fruit, but a bad tree bears bad fruit."

So there are two kinds of fruit, good and bad. My grandmother had a crabapple tree. We kids ate the apples, but they were terrible. My grandmother warned us to limit how many we ate to avoid stomach aches. Crabapples are bad fruit, not good fruit like the apples you buy in the store.

More particularly, what then is spiritual fruit? The Bible talks a lot about this and calls it our works, or rather what we do. Like apple trees, there are both good fruit and bad fruit. Fruit is another term for "our works." Our works are either good or bad.

When you study through prayer, God tells us good spiritual fruit has two components. First, it is only done through God's power. Jesus said He only did what He saw the Father do. In other words, it was God's power working through Him. If I do something by my own strength, then I did it and not God. I get the credit, not God. Good fruit gives God the credit. Bad fruit is everything else. Now there are a lot of things I have the power to do. But the strength or determination comes from God. Although I can do it, the reason I do it because of Him.

A sidebar comment is we should be careful to not steal God's glory on what He does. It is so easy to take credit for His works. This makes God mad. He doesn't like it when He's a theft victim.

The second component is motive. Godly motives produce good fruit. There are three components to a godly motive: love of God, love of your neighbor, and love of the brethren. If your intention is to look out for the best interests of God, your neighbor, or other believers, then you can say there is a godly motive is behind what you do. Another clue—if you do something to get something out of it, such as credit, then it is not a godly motive.

Looking out for others' eternal fruit is an active expression of the love for the brethren.

We are complex creatures, complicating everything. I have never done anything without me getting at least a little something. Likewise, I have never done anything without at least a little of my own power in it.

One year I planted a garden and planted some cucumbers and squash. The bees cross-pollinated them, and they both tasted rather funny. I have heard of people planting cucumbers next to jalapeno peppers, hoping to make hot cucumbers. I am like hot cucumbers—a little of me and a little of God.

I can inspire others to have godly works with godly motives. I can do this by listening to them, talking with them, and praying for them. I can share relevant scriptures. Most importantly, I can stay in the background. Most likely, if I am in the center, I get the praise of men. The praise of men is definitely not conducive to eternal fruit.

It is important to have good works or fruit in eternity. Scripture talks about our works being judged, and I think the offering or gifts we bring in eternity will be our fruits. I want to give God a lot of offerings, and I want others to do the same.

Scripture talks about the riches of heaven. This is our fruit or works. I want to be rich throughout eternity. Few of us say we are rich in this life. But all of us can be rich in eternity, and it lasts a lot longer.

Acts 1:8 tells us we are witnesses to Jesus everywhere we go. God sees even our secret things. May our secrets be good fruit!

What are some examples of good fruit? You are walking somewhere and see some trash. Picking it up (especially if no one notices) could be a good work. Being pleasant counts as a good work, especially if others are nasty. Talking about nothing of importance with someone with no friends is a good work.

But the big fruit is what you do for your enemies. Your enemies are those people who hate you for no good reason, or maybe they have a good reason. I don't understand why my enemies hate me. As far as I know, I did nothing bad to these people, but they hated me anyway. I try to be pleasant and treat them with the same respect and dignity I want to be treated with. It is so hard to not retaliate when they attack. I should mention retaliation is polite, but as real as punching someone out.

How well do I do? Rather badly, actually. You might pray for me. We can pray for each other to do what God wants. Sharing scripture does something to both the listener and the speaker to encourage both to please God more, if only so slightly. Just don't be obnoxious.

Much of the time we will not see our fruit until we get to eternity. It is certain we will all get there. I vainly tried talking to someone once in hospice. I don't understand him at all. In a short time, he would be in eternity. I thought he would be at least a little curious about what eternity would be like.

We are discussing your fruit, not mine. I want you to have as much fruit as possible. I want you to be as wealthy as possible for all of eternity. I am looking out for your best interests. The apostle Paul wrote in a similar manner in Colossians 1:28–29 (NKJV), "Him we preach, warning every man and teaching every man in all wisdom, that we may present every man perfect in Christ Jesus. To this *end* I also labor, striving according to His working which works in me mightily."

I believe God will give me fruit for helping others gain fruit.

In my mind, everything starts with being drawn to Jesus. It is not going to church but sensing an inner need for God. All of us need to be loved in a way no one can fill except Jesus. We try all kinds of things, and from my experience, it all fails. It all falls short. There must be something pulling us toward Jesus. Most of what we call witnessing is this. We are making it easier for the Holy Spirit to draw someone. Unless the Holy Spirit draws someone, he or she can't be drawn. When someone responds to the Holy Spirit's drawing him or her, regardless of where he or she is in his or her spiritual walk, it is fruit.

First Corinthians 12:3b (NKJV) says, "No one can say that Jesus is Lord except by the Holy Spirit."

So the things we do and say help draw others. Also, when we pray, we encourage the Holy Spirit to draw someone. Prayer is an important but overlooked fruit.

Part of the Holy Spirit's drawing results in a deep-seated conviction of personal sin and unworthiness. Only the Holy Spirit can convict this way. If I tell someone he or she is a pitiful example of humanity, it only causes trouble—even if it is true! The Holy Spirit works on and from the inside. A friend told me of when he was convicted he was a sinner, he wanted to jump from a building, but the building he was on wasn't high enough and no building was high enough. I saw myself as a pitiful, pathetic, loser and wept. Only God could have shown myself at such a deep level.

At some point in this process, an individual comes to a crisis point, a window of decision. They will either decide to live for Jesus, or they will decide to reject Him. It has no relationship to whether they are church members or if they walked an aisle, prayed a prayer, signed a card, were baptized, became active in their church, or all the other religious stuff we do. It is a decision on which kingdom will they live in: God's or the world's.

Their cry to God converts them in their window of decision. Their cry must only be to sincerely decide to live for Jesus, believing He died on the cross for their sins and is alive, while confessing His name. Jesus enters the core of their being, the place motivating and creating desires. For most of us, the external transformation may not be dramatic. Some people are so thoroughly convinced that the transformation is spectacular.

I didn't realize how impressive my conversion was. Several

years later, my boss's boss called me into his office, shut the door, and commented on the change.

The church or denomination doesn't matter if Jesus is preached and Him crucified and resurrected.

Paul said in 1 Corinthians 2:2 (NKJV), "For I determined not to know anything among you except Jesus Christ and Him crucified."

There is enough in this verse to keep us busy studying for a long time. Paul is saying Jesus the Christ is the foundation. Scripture says Christ means a lot more than someone's last name. It is a Greek word referring to the anointed one. All of the Old Testament, in one way or another, points to the Christ. It is not the Christ baby like we have at Christmas, although the Old Testament mentions the child. It is a powerful yet absolutely humble conqueror, God Himself, the Creator, the one who holds it all together. It is the focus of all history.

In talking about Jesus crucified, we are talking about God paying the full price for everything we did. We are talking about the righteousness of Christ covering us. It involves the love of Jesus, His resurrection, and His return.

Once a person is in the kingdom of God, he or she must learn how to live there. Everyone I know is at a different place in the process, and ideally, we help each other. I listen to preachers and friends, read books, study, and apply myself to learn what this Christian life is all about.

What does all this have to do with fruit? Every time I do something to promote each of these steps, by the power and love of God, I inspire fruit for the kingdom. One day I was working with a fellow Christian, who came to me and said,

"That guy over there wants to talk to me." I only said, "So talk to him." He did and wound up leading the man to Jesus.

I encouraged my friend to do the work of the kingdom. In a tiny way, I inspired him to have kingdom fruit.

Helping someone understand Scripture or prayer helps him or her grow fruit for eternity. God gave me influence with several people. Using my influence to encourage them for Jesus is part of this ambition.

I don't need the limelight, be the hero, or do the work getting the fruit. I only have to help others do what God wants, which will get them fruit.

It's not restricted to believers. One of my former coworkers complained about another coworker who he says, "won't give upon his soul."

A word of encouragement, thanks, or helpfulness can help others in a critical way. I wish I were better at this.

But this ambition is not "control." If I am trying to control others, to make them think like me, go to my church, or have my opinion, it is worldly fruit, not godly fruit. People using scripture to beat others over the head are not making good fruit but bad fruit. I don't want to argue with someone to prove my point but rather point him or her to the truth inherent in Jesus.

A friend does not believe in the Trinity. Once he wanted to argue about it. I tried several times to end our conversation, but he didn't let it drop. Finally, we stopped. He was mad, and I was sad. In our conversation, my friend was not interested in what was right or wrong, only trying to get me to his point of view. If it had been a rational discussion, instead of the name-calling he indulged in, we could both been edified and more educated. Instead, fellowship was broken. Instead of fruit, he sowed condemnation.

Sometimes it is necessary to be silent. I read a testimony by a lady who decided if a young man said one word on the ride home from an evangelistic crusade, she would decide against Jesus forever. He was silent, she became a believer, and now they're married. He sowed fruit in this lady because he followed the gentle wind of the Holy Spirit and said nothing.

I have been speaking on what fruit is, how to get it, and examples. Let's take a couple of minutes and think about specific action items.

The tree analogy is good. If you have a fruit tree, you ensure sure it has the proper amount of water and sunshine. You fertilize it and spray it for insects and diseases. You carefully watch the flowers and the fruit's development. It angers you if birds or raccoons steal your fruit. At the perfect moment, when the fruit is ripe, but not overripe, you harvest.

It is the same with this spiritual ambition. I water it with godly friends, fertilize it with the word, and bask in the sunshine of God's presence. I deal with the insects and diseases of my sinful desires by giving them to God. It angers me when Satan steals my fruit. I must do something. It might mean I put myself in places where I am less likely to be tempted. At the perfect moment, God harvests the fruit. I give Him permission by trying to not rush Him or delay Him.

These are different ways to talk about obedience. I learn a lot about obeying God from scripture. I start with what I know and try to learn more. I will let God change me. This ambition helps water, fertilize, and encourage others. I am helping them grow by being a friend. I think about what tempts people and don't let my freedom take away their liberty. There are many things in themselves that are neither good nor bad. A new car may be one of those. I don't brag about getting a new car (which only happens every ten to twelve years) because others might not afford one. There is nothing wrong with a new car, unless it plunges you into the bondage of debt. By the way, debt is a major trap in this country. It is one of the main reasons we have so many troubles.

I want to tie this part of my personal ambition with the previous three ambitions. The first, God's presence, is the foundation of spirituality, which is the only thing able to fill my heart's spiritual hole. From His presence, I receive the selfless love I crave, the love that loves me no matter what I have done, or where I have been. He doesn't care if I wear a suit or shackles. I tried filling my spiritual hole with all kinds of things and thought about trying many others, but nothing else works. This need, for the love of God that can only come from God, is as strong perhaps stronger now as a Christian, as I allow it to mold me.

Write down what you believe is God's ambition for you personally, not what some preacher says, but what God is saying to you personally. Then start doing those things that make it possible for God to work. Most likely it will include listening carefully to God, reading the Bible, prayer, and other spiritual disciplines. How and what you do to put it into place requires insight from God.

And that leads to the second aspect of this ambition, to be filled with God's love. This is not a casual thing, but to be so filled up it is overflowing. I don't want love I must work at generating, I want the kind of love that naturally bubbles up from inside, an important part of spiritual strength.

But love needs direction, which is my ambition's third aspect. I can do what God wants by hearing the gentle wind of the Holy Spirit. I can do what God wants. I cannot do everything I think of but need to focus on those things pleasing to God. Even then, there are way too many possibilities. How should I choose? The only way to build fruit for eternity is to follow God's plan for me, and the gentle wind of the Holy Spirit is my guide. He is often quiet, but if I am careful and listen closely, I can still hear Him.

I know for a fact God wants all His people to be rich in eternity. Matthew 6:19–20 (NKJV) says, "Do not lay up for yourselves treasures on earth, where moth and rust destroy and where thieves break in and steal; but lay up for yourselves treasures in heaven, where neither moth nor rust destroys and where thieves do not break in and steal."

Eternity's wealth is the fruit from our works. I am building treasure by my helping others to gain fruit. It reminds me of my sister. Several years ago, we bought all our Christmas gifts, wrapped them, and put them in a bag on my parents' porch. Sis rented a Santa's suit and handed out all the gifts. Every Christmas, she still hands out the gifts, although without the suit. She gets tremendous pleasure in giving gifts, even if she didn't buy them. God gets a similar (but more complete and holy) pleasure when He hands out fruit in eternity. He wants to give everyone so much, and all that is stopping Him is us. The more fruit you get, the more pleased God becomes.

It makes me happy to please God. It is what I, to a major extent, live for.

Yet, I won't know how much fruit others are getting until I get to eternity. Right now, I trudge onward, doing my small part where I can. Rarely someone tells me how much something I said or did meant to them.

Jesus fed thousands, and then he ministered with 120 disciples. Their numbers dwindled to 12, one of whom betrayed him. Of the 11, He took 3 deep into the garden to pray with him, and they fell asleep. While He died on the cross, only John was there, and he stood at a distance. Jesus did not find out how much fruit He caused people to have until He got to eternity, and scripture says it is millions (Rev. 7:9). I am no better than my Master (John 13:16), so I should not expect to see what I have done until I get to eternity.

I have been talking about helping others get more fruit, but I want to take a minute and ask where you stand. Are you realizing how far from God you are, and do you want to do something about it? The only way to get closer to God is to pray. Tell him you are far from Him, and ask Him to be closer. God looks at the intent of your heart rather than your precise words.

7

Inner Spiritual Peace

Let's review my spiritual ambition list:

- To feel God's presence
- To be filled with God's love
- To sense the gentle wind of God
- To inspire others to obtain fruit for God's kingdom
- To have inner spiritual peace
- To have boldness to do as I hear
- To be used with power
- To see the times

We addressed presence, being filled with God's love, sensing the gentle wind of God, and inspiring others to obtain fruit. These are the basics of faith. I remind the reader these things are a pyramid, starting with the presence of God as the foundation. Without Him, we have nothing.

Next is inner spiritual peace. As I began studying spiritual peace, I initially thought it was easy. After all, who doesn't want peace in his or her heart? Yet, it is the most difficult so far, taking me two years to grapple with it.

Why is spiritual peace so difficult? I think there are three main reasons. First, we struggle with it as much as anything, whether we admit it or not. We all want peace, but it is as elusive as a gentle breeze on a hot summer day. Even the most devout believer struggles with inner peace.

Second, we confuse inner spiritual peace with contentment. The Bible doesn't help much here either, since Paul said he has learned to be content in all things (see Philippians 4:10). We all want and need contentment. However, rich celebrities amaze me. They have everything. They have money, fame, and the easy lifestyle. They can live anywhere, buy any house they want, or drive any car. They don't even have to drive, as they can hire someone to drive them. They are always welcome at endless parties. Yet how often do we read about one of them committing suicide? All the "everything" they have is not enough. They lack contentment.

Contentment and peace overlap. There is contentment in the peace I am referring to, but this peace is much more. It is in this "much more" that sets it apart and is the confusing part.

Third, you find apparent contradictions when you search scriptures. In Matthew 10:34 (NKJV), Jesus said: "Do not think that I came to bring peace on earth. I did not come to bring peace but a sword."

The angel, when announcing the birth of Jesus, said in Luke 2:14 (NKJV), "Glory to God in the highest, And on earth peace, goodwill toward men!"

Yet we read in John 20:19 (NKJV), speaking after the resurrection of Jesus: "Then, the same day at evening, being the first *day* of the week, when the doors were shut where the disciples were assembled, for fear of the Jews, Jesus came and stood in the midst, and said to them, 'Peace *be* with you.'"

This sounds like a contradiction. On one hand, scripture says we will have peace, and on the other hand, it says we will not have peace. We must look deeper, hoping to resolve this apparent contradiction. Let me be explicit. There is no contradiction. Both statements are true, and we can trust them.

Peace is a difficult concept. Generally, we think of peace as what happens after two warring countries decide to not be at war. War is when one country tries to destroy another. Peace is when they don't try to destroy each other. The same concept applies to people. We all know how the behavior of two people at war is different than when there is peace.

But at this basic level, there are different kinds of war and peace, confusing the difference. In the 1960s we heard a lot about the cold war, which both the United States and Russia made provisions to destroy each other. They were at war but never fired shots. There were the times when we supported opposite sides of a civil war. I never really understood the Cold War. I suspect it was an opportunity to play with our fancy new war toys.

Sometimes we are at peace with others. However, our peace is more like a ceasefire. We don't help each other. We act as if the other does not exist. We go about our business, and they go about theirs. We minimize mutual interactions. We may only tolerate them. An acquaintance told me he and his wife tolerated each other. Were they at war or at peace? I find his relationship with his wife miserable.

These concepts apply to nations, companies, families, and every kind of human interaction. Many churches tolerate each other, or perhaps act as if the others don't exist. All of us have experienced or are experiencing these different scenarios, and perhaps even more.

Somebody sent me a new serenity prayer: Give me the patience to put up with stupid people, the self-control to not respond, and the wisdom to know that if I do what I want to do, I will go to jail.

So, what is this thing called peace, and why is it so difficult?

Peace means rest, safe, happy, good health, reward, rest, restitution, prosperity, and a gift, and scripture uses it in all these ways.

Peace usually means absence of conflict between two people. But there are different kinds of relationships. For example, there is one relationship between me and other humans, another between me and God, a third between me and the devil, and finally one between me and myself. Scripture addresses all of these.

The angels, when they announced the birth of Jesus and Jesus after the resurrection addressed the most important one, peace between God and people. Scripture says our sin is nothing more than rebellion, and rebellion is a form of war. This war is a war to the death. There are no prisoners, nor will any escape. We will lose. But God took pity on us, and Jesus came that we might have peace in our war with God.

Jesus said in John 14:27 (NKJV), "Peace I leave with you, my peace I give to you; not as the world gives do I give to you. Let not your heart be troubled, neither let it be afraid." The peace Jesus is talking about is primarily the one between us and God, but also the others. We can rest (which is hard) in knowing that Jesus is in control. Circumstances may not look like it, but in the end, God wins. It is like a sports game. The home team is behind, but in the last quarter, they put their star player in and give him special plays. Between his abilities and new plays, the home team wins. You can have confidence on your team if you know the strategy, and this is God's strategy. In the last quarter, right at the end, Jesus is coming back and bringing with Himself the host of angels and absolute authority. He conquerors His opponents with his word (see Rev. 19:15). His people are "in the know" and can have confidence in both Jesus's return and His ultimate victory, regardless of the current score. We can have confidence to trust in this ultimate victory while all types of conflict rage around us.

Paul said in Romans 8:6–7 (NKJV), "For to be carnally minded *is* death, but to be spiritually minded *is* life and peace. Because the carnal mind *is* enmity against God; for it is not subject to the law of God, nor indeed can be."

Carnally minded is our natural mind. It's the part of our thinking by nature. Enmity means hostility and hatred. This passage tells us that by nature, we are hostile to God and hate him. It also refers to being spiritually minded. We are not naturally spiritually minded. Jesus gives us spiritual minds when we make Jesus Lord.

Within every believer are both a natural mind and a spiritual mind. The two are at war. Now we all know nothing is more powerful than God. He will win.

But sometimes it seems different in our hearts. There is an old story about how we have two dogs in us, one good and one bad. They are constantly fighting. The one we feed is the one that wins.

How do we help our spiritual mind to win? Everything we look at feeds our mind. Everything we read, hear, or say feeds our mind. This is why Bible reading and prayer help our spiritual mind. Scripture modifies what we think, say, and do. These disciplines, along with others like worship, etc., feed our spiritual mind. The good things feed the part of us dedicated to Jesus, while the bad feed our evil nature.

To have victory, we need to trust, obey God, and actively love. Daily, every one of us have issues providing us with yet more opportunities to trust God. We hear bad news, see bad things, and experience bad things. Sometimes it is difficult to have trust. Once a drug dealer threatened me. Fortunately, God took over, and I didn't realize how serious it was until later. Loved ones die or are destroyed by all kinds of things. Children leave home. Painful hurts fill life. In all these things, we know that God is greater, and we can use each to trust Him more. Each victory brings us closer to God, feeding our spiritual minds.

We need to obey. When we realize God is telling us to do something, we need to obey. I don't need a supernatural manifestation to know God's will for so many things. It is God's will that I be subject to authorities. It means I don't rock the boat and I try to do what they want if it is not illegal or immoral. The Bible gives us plenty to work on. Scripture gives us plenty of things to obey God, like patience, longsuffering, forgiving each other, looking out for each other's best interest, honoring those in authority, and so forth. God also gives us direction on a personal level. He may use any of the ways I discussed in the chapter on sensing the gentle wind of God to direct us. Regardless of the means he chooses, we need to be quick to obey.

I want to discuss one more way to have spiritual peace. We need to go about our business manifesting love. Scripture says we are to love God with everything we have, love our neighbors as we love ourselves, and love fellow believers as Jesus has loved us. More difficult, Jesus told us to love our enemies.

It does not mean we tell them, "Have a nice day, you dirty scumbag."

Love means putting their best interests above our own.

But we are still in a war with the devil. Paul tells us how to wage war in Ephesians 6:11–17 (NKJV):

> Put on the whole armor of God, that you may be able to stand against the wiles of the devil. For we do not wrestle against flesh and blood, but against principalities, against powers, against the rulers of the darkness of this age, against spiritual *hosts* of wickedness in the heavenly *places*. Therefore take up the whole armor of God, that you may be able to withstand in the evil day, and having done all, to stand. Stand therefore, having girded your waist with truth, having put on the breastplate of righteousness, and having shod your feet with the preparation of the gospel of peace; above all, taking the shield of faith with which you will be able to quench all the fiery darts of the wicked one. And

> take the helmet of salvation, and the sword of
> the Spirit, which is the word of God.

We could spend a lot of time talking about this, and it is worthy of meditating on. The point is we are in a serious war, and God has given to us tools to allow us to win. Those tools are: truth, righteousness, good news of peace, faith, salvation, and the word of God.

One of those tools is the good news of peace. We are in a war, yet a powerful tool is the news of peace. This important tool is peace between God and man. Fundamentally, man struggles to find peace. I have heard it said every culture has spiritual components. Everyone everywhere is trying to make peace with God. I was surprised once to hear a man who worships nature talk about the need to purify himself. I wanted to tell him that he needed to do something about his sin. Fortunately, God has already sent Jesus to the cross to do something about our sin

The devil uses the world system and our own sins against us. His tools are ego, pleasure, self-serving attitudes, hatred, love of riches, greed, oppression, unrighteous anger, and so on. His most powerful tool is deception. This will make me happy. This is what I want. These lies are endless, and what we think we want will often end up destroying us.

The devil uses words to destroy us. He will whisper in our ear, "We are no good, we can't do it, they don't like me" (as if it matters), or whatever button we have. He knows our buttons and pushes them.

What did God do about it? First John 1:8–9 (NKJV) says, "If we say that we have no sin, we deceive ourselves, and the truth is not in us. If we confess our sins, He is faithful and just to forgive us *our* sins and to cleanse us from all unrighteousness."

We sin, and God forgives us. When the devil traps me I and do wrong, I must admit it to God, and He will forgive me. It is never too late. There is always forgiveness from God available to me and everyone else.

Inner peace does not mean I won't have war, for I struggle to trust God. I struggle to live like God wants me to. But it does mean God and I have peace. There is no war between us. Jesus finished our war on the cross. I accepted the terms of peace when I made Jesus Lord.

But it means more than that we are not actively attacking each other. It means God is actively helping me with my struggles. We are not preparing to attack each other, nor are we tolerating each other. I do admit the best I can do is tolerate some people. Tolerating them is not God's plan.

It means I have rest if the spiritual war between God and me is finished. The whole book of Galatians talks about how we have rested from trying to please God by doing good things. It is not saying we don't do good things, but instead saying doing good will not, by itself, win God's favor.

Several years ago, I mentioned to a coworker that I was a boring person. She disagreed with me and commented on how exciting my life is. I thought about it and decided she was right—living for God is exciting. Now I believe I'm a boring person living an exciting life.

Let me summarize. Spiritual peace is peace between God and me, bringing with it many benefits. My part is to first make Jesus my Lord, which I do by deciding to follow Him, confessing Him freely, and believing Jesus is raised from the dead (see

Roman 9:9–10). Second, I must trust God in everything, obey Him in everything, and love God, my neighbor, and my fellow believers.

Peace is different from contentment, although they overlap. While the war between me and God is over, the war between my humanity and my spirituality and me and the devil intensified. But when my life is over, Jesus has already won, meaning our enemies are vanquished. They don't accept it yet. They will.

Perhaps you have never made peace with God. Now is a good time. Perhaps you did, but you have drifted away. Now is a good time to renew your commitment. Perhaps you are struggling and don't think you have inner peace. Now is a good time to enlist God's help. Only you know whether you have ever made peace with God or need to renew your commitment. I daresay if Paul struggled with the war between his natural and spiritual minds (see Romans 7:22–25), all of us struggle.

In every case, we address this with prayer, and basically the prayer is the same for those who never had peace, those needing to renew their commitment to Jesus and regain their peace, and those simply struggling. We admit our status, ask God to forgive us, make Jesus Lord, believe Jesus is alive, and confess Him as our Lord to men.

8

Boldness to Do as I Hear

Previous chapters dealt briefly on God's presence, being filled with God's love, sensing the gentle wind of God, and inspiring others to obtain kingdom fruit. These are the basics of faith. I should mention these ambitions are a pyramid, starting with the presence of God. Without Him, we have nothing. Then I addressed inner spiritual peace. Peace is more complex than I initially thought, involving a huge swath of my Christian walk.

Today I want to discuss boldness but most particularly, the boldness to do as I hear God speak.

It is easy to have boldness in a crazy way. Most outlaw motorcyclists would be offended if you hinted they did not have boldness. This comes from the belief that the opposite of boldness is a coward.

The Bible says we should be doers of the Word, not hearers only (James 1:22).

This sounds easy, but when we look closely, it is not. For example, we must know the Word to be a doer of the Word.

We must be willing to apply the Word to daily life, even when it costs me.

I had a tax audit. After I reviewed my documentation for the audit, I determined I made a $200 error. It would have been easy to fudge the numbers, and the auditor could not have found the fudge. I admit I was tempted. But I decided God didn't want me to be that kind of person, so not only did I provide the correct information, but I also pointed out the error to the auditor. I'm not saying everyone should do this, but I am saying I thought God wanted me to. I personally heard this based on my understanding of God's kingdom principles. As an aside, the auditor didn't know how to respond and eventually issued me a five-dollar fine.

Scripture clearly gives us many examples in daily life. Telling the truth, loving, being kind, looking out for our fellow man, and so on are clearly stated. I will never be able to say I have these clearly stated points totally mastered.

But to make matters worse, there are more things we do that are not written in scripture. For example, what should I order in a restaurant? Most of the time it doesn't matter, but one time God specifically told me to order the BBQ chicken. I argued with Him and told Him I don't like chicken. But I ordered it anyway and found out I liked BBQ chicken. My obedience was very small, but I had to boldly be obedient.

This almost silly example has several points worth talking about. First, it didn't matter if I ate the chicken or the burger, other than obedience. Yet God spoke to me. I heard Him and had to obey. Obedience is key and the most important part of this little story. He was telling me to do something for my pleasure rather than some great spiritual good (showing how

God loves us even in the minutiae of life). I found out I liked BBQ chicken. I have ordered it many times since without the Holy Spirit's prompting.

If God is interested in BBQ, how much more is He interested in greater things? It may cost us something in this life. When we get to eternity I believe we may understand the importance of things seemingly without value, but we did them obediently, or worse, didn't do them or did them half-heartedly.

There is another point. I rarely hear from God about what to order in a restaurant. But I was listening. I was ready to hear from God. We must be ready to hear from God at all times. I like to say "have our spiritual antennae up and on."

Now some things are easy to obey. Ordering a meal is easy. But we are constantly faced with life-changing decisions. Some are about the things of life, like which car to buy, job to take, or spouse to marry. We have opinions, usually passionately. I liked a girl in college. I would have done anything or gone anywhere for her. Yet, it would have been a disaster if we became more serious. I see so many young people not willing to have the boldness to do what God says. A young man becomes enamored with a cute chick. One thing leads to another, and they get together. The problem is God was never a part of their thinking, and yet, they often blame God when it turns out badly. This is strange, because it wasn't his idea at all!

Maybe God does want the two of them to get together. But they don't have the courage to wait. By running ahead of God, they miss His perfect timing. Again, things don't turn out the best they could have.

Maybe God's plan is for the two of them to get together, and maybe they wait for the right time. But they may still have left God out of all the decisions, and they are the worst. They acted legalistically or from a human standpoint and not out of obedience based on the love of God.

Being bold means having a strong and vibrant testimony proclaiming you have a new life because Jesus is alive. It is supernatural, involving Jesus in every decision you make. I am continually surprised at the seemingly small things that have major impact on someone. I spent an hour with someone just goofing off. Later I found out he was very depressed, and it meant a lot to him that I spent time with him.

Another part of boldness is to look for those opportunities. A bold person steps out, not hesitant, when he knows he should move. I hear about brave souls diving from cliffs two hundred or more feet in the air. I think they have a form of bravery. But they will not jump off a two hundred–foot cliff onto a pavement. Boldness does not lead to stupidity.

Sometimes God wants you to tell someone what God has done for you. You may be justifiably afraid of the response. Once you hear God wants you to move forward, you do must so without hesitation. Like those cliff jumpers diving from two hundred feet into a lake, you can't stop halfway. Serving Jesus is all or nothing. Paul was constantly being beat up or imprisoned for telling people Jesus died for their sins and rose again so they might have new life. He also asked other believers to pray he could have boldness. I don't feel so badly when I realize Paul struggled with boldness as well.

Sometimes it is not clear what we should do, but we know the consequences are severe. A friend received a call from someone about to commit suicide. What would you say if it happened to you? The standard kind of answer is to tell him he has a lot to live for and so on. My friend, however, did what God wanted him to do. He told the caller to go ahead.

The caller was shocked, and asked, "Don't you care?"

My friend answered by saying, "Of course I care, but it is your life. I just want to tell you what is on the other side so you can make a rational decision."

He then told him about the lost going to hell and Jesus died to prevent it, and the caller can have a new life because Jesus is alive. This was what the caller wanted, a different life. He found a new life in Jesus. Now, I don't recommend this approach at all, unless God directly speaks to you.

Boldness is not restricted to saying things. After all, every politician says many things. It is living it. Sometimes we must trust God and not say or do something. Silence, if directed by Jesus, can be very powerful.

Let us delve deeper. Boldness is following Jesus no matter what. It comes from within. It is not something we decide when confronted with decisions, but it wells up within us. It is what we are as much as what we do or don't do. I believe it is one of the main fruits we will receive in eternity.

So how do you get boldness. First, you can't by yourself. All you can do is give God permission to give it to you. It is a supernatural act. Typically, God will give you boldness in an area where you are naturally lacking. The Bible says, "In our weakness He is strong" (2 Corinthians 12:9).

To give God permission, we must first tell Him we want boldness. Then we open our soul's most intimate parts to Him. He rummages around, dusts this, throws junk out, and basically cleans up the joint. He doesn't change our basic personality; after all, He created it for us. But He fixes the broken parts of our spirit and our soul.

We must be broken. We can't do it ourselves. We need the supernatural power of God. Peter could never preach his Pentecost sermon without first being convinced he didn't have that ability in himself, or without the power of the Holy Spirit. His brokenness from denying Jesus three times during Jesus's trial humbled him enough that Peter could be used mightily. He stood up and boldly proclaimed what Jesus had done, and thousands believed. Moreover, he did it to the same crowd that wanted Jesus nailed to the cross. Whatever else you say, you must admit Peter was gutsy.

We must let the Holy Spirit be the generator powering supernatural acts. You are reflecting the love God has for the one you are witnessing to. Remember, much of witnessing is not verbal. At the right time, God will prompt you to provide the verbal witness. Don't forget, the Holy Spirit is a person, as well as God, and not some supernatural force we can use as we want to use.

If the Holy Spirit talks to you, you need to both hear and understand. A life of prayer is the only way to be familiar with His voice. We can pray while we mow the grass, take a shower, or lay down to sleep. No one needs to know you are in communion with God. It can become second nature.

The more we obey, the more boldness we have. Doing little things God wants trains us to do the bigger things.

Then there is the preparation. We don't know what God would have us say to someone, so we must prepare. This means we study the Bible. We seek God's understanding and let different passages come alive. The side benefit is we are changed as well. We get something out of Bible study and often may not know what we get. Then, when we talk with someone, the Holy Spirit brings to our minds passages as needed. Using scripture, under the Holy Spirit, brings great power to our witness.

God does not respect persons. He wants everyone in the kingdom. If you have something against someone, you are frustrating the Holy Spirit, and you'll have limited spiritual impact. Your boldness becomes foolishness.

Scripture says we should come boldly before the throne of God, presenting our requests. We have become lazy and self-serving with our prayers. We don't realize the tremendous privilege and great blessing God gave us to be able to pray to God. He lets us know He listens to our prayers. Now my prayers are not eloquent or even adequate. They are like me trying to give the president of the United States advice. I am not up to the task. But the Holy Spirit translates our prayers, particularly when we pray from selfless love.

We think we have done too much, fallen so far, or lost opportunities to have God listen to us. We think we are too much of a sinner. I have some news for you. First John 1:9 tells us if we confess our sins, He will forgive us and cleanse us. We always have sin, but primarily our actions are not in the way. Our ego and pride are. We often take God for granted. These are the things hindering our prayers, as well as how we treat people or rather our relationships.

Being bold to do as I hear is like the summation of so much of Christianity. I heard of a teacher in Soviet Russia who served God in her heart but not with her life. Being bold is an all-or-nothing thing. Many Christians around the world are considered dead by their nonbelieving families after deciding to believe. Their families have funerals for them and bury a casket with a tombstone, marking that this child has become a believer and is therefore dead to them. Some feel obligated to beat or kill the believer. It is not easy to become a Christian in those areas of the world.

The Bible says there is a special reward for them.

Do you want boldness? Do you want more boldness? I don't have nearly enough.

You can pray for me to have more boldness in the Holy Spirit.

Where do you stand? Now is a good time to talk to God about it.

In every case, we address this with prayer, and basically the prayer is the same for all who want boldness, exercising boldness, or getting more boldness. Basically, we admit our spiritual state to God, believing Jesus is both Lord and risen from the dead, and telling Him we want boldness. Then, we act when we hear God's whisper.

9

To Be Used with Power

Now I'll address my spiritual ambition number 7, which is to be used with power. I delayed working on this one because of the personal price.

Many put God's power at the head of their list. My concern is different. I want to serve God with power, but the flashy aspects are of no interest to me. I am happy when I pray and someone gets healed. But there are many more important things. I fear the warning from 1 Corinthians 13:1–3. This passage tells us no matter what we do, to the point of delivering our bodies to be burned, it is meaningless without love. I want love to be paramount, and I have a lot of room for improvement in the love department.

For the record, the love Paul talks about is the selfless love God has for us, where He loves us and gets essentially nothing in return.

As I studied spiritual power, I discovered it is my hardest ambition, both to study and to apply. I know it requires giving control of my life to Jesus. It is not limited to external control but the deepest essence of who I am, so deep that only God knows what is down there. This spiritual power energizes other ambitions, so maybe it does belong near the pyramid's top.

When we think of power, what comes to our minds? I admire the top-end Porsche, which has more horsepower than I have money. The shuttle, as it takes off, displays great power. I regret never seeing a launch. The sun, a giant, fiery furnace, has unbelievable power. An asteroid smashing into the earth, killing almost every living thing, has unimaginable power. Stars and galaxies collide, unleashing forces far beyond our understanding.

There are other kinds of power. A little newborn has great power over its mother; watch her jump when it cries. Political leaders have the power to wage war, and business leaders change the economy's course. All these have great power, and there are most likely many others you can think of.

Now I want to address the greatest power—spiritual power. It manifests itself in many different ways. For power to show itself, it must oppose something else. Spiritual power opposes the devil, the world, and our flesh. The main tools of the opposition are deception, possessions, and lust, which include more than merely sexual lust. Lust includes the desires for all kinds of pleasure, possessions, and power. The devil, the world, and our flesh all work together. Their objective is to kill, steal, and destroy (see John 10:10).

Spiritual power is what we use when we fight the devil's deception, the world's attractions, and our sinful human desires. Spiritual power means when you pray, you get answers. People are convicted when you tell them of Jesus. It means giving up your sins and becoming far more Christlike.

Spiritual power means there is no argument that can stand before you. It is as if God himself is present, and in fact He is. It means my life becomes more meaningful than I could ever imagine. It means I have an excitement in all parts of life, coupled with unbelievable joy. It means people see my life and want their lives to be like mine. But most of all, it means putting our sinful self to death and allowing Jesus to resurrect new life in us on a continual basis.

True spiritual power is the power to live a changed life. How is it changed? It becomes more servantlike and filled with selfless love, as described in 1 Corinthians 13. It is primarily spiritual, not physical. It is eternal, not temporary. It is, purely and simply, the deepest manifestation of the Holy Spirit.

Spiritual power is not limited to speaking and doing God's directives. It is being like God with similar impact. It is not sensational entertainment, like King Herod wanted when he tried Jesus. It is changing myself to become more like Jesus. I can't look at the results to know if I was used with God's power, but instead, I must look at myself. Did I have motivation based on love or anything else?

The purpose of spiritual power is to be a witness to Jesus. Jesus gave this charter in Acts 1:8 (NKJV): "But you shall receive power when the Holy Spirit has come upon you; and you shall be witnesses to Me in Jerusalem, and in all Judea and Samaria, and to the end of the earth."

Note that He said to be a witness to Him, not for Him. The audience is no one less than God Himself. In legal terms, a witness is before a judge giving testimony. We are before the perfect Judge, Jesus, giving our testimony. This testimony is then used by God to convict the lost. This conviction leads to faith. It is outside this scope to do more than mention Hebrews 11:1 uses conviction instead of substance in some translations.

There are many spiritual tools available to us. Prayer, fellowship, and scripture reading are so commonly talked about that I can add nothing, except to say these foundational basics reveal what we need for the other tools. Without trying to make one tool more important than another (or limit to only these tools), I want to discuss intimacy, knowledge, purity, surrender (of control), faith, devotion, and love.

Spiritual power is all about advancing God's kingdom, first in my life and then in the lives around me. This process is ultimately about my heart and soul and the hearts and souls of those around us. I believe our will is the most stubborn, impenetrable, and immovable object in existence. One of the greatest mysteries is why (and even how) God gave us free will. But give He did, and now our will is the prize. Some of the potential side benefits are a special relationship with God Himself, salvation, and all the good things God brings into our lives. Spiritual power is about bending our will to God.

We all use the free will God gave us to make many spiritual decisions. Ultimately and individually, we make decisions, but spiritual power helps us make clear decisions, instead of ones clouded by confusing noises.

I want spiritual power. I have some, but I want more. What do you want? What will you pay for it? This power costs everything I have.

Ultimately the Holy Spirit is the conduit from the Father, to us, for all spiritual power. This power is available to us because Jesus died on the cross and resurrected from the dead, but most importantly, because He is now at the right hand of the Father making intercession for us (see Romans 8:34). As our advocate (or better understood, lawyer), He is using our testimony in God's court.

For completeness's sake, the devil also has evil spiritual power. It is corrupted and certainly weaker than the Lord's. Instead of bringing life, it brings death, and so forth. Our fallen nature makes the devil's power attractive to us, despite its weaknesses. This is often our spiritual battle. But let us not be confused by this, and for the rest of this discussion, I'm only talking about the God's spiritual power.

Ultimately, we must be broken. This is the only starting point for serious spiritual power. I have seen it in my life. God uses me more after I realize I am a loser, professionally, socially, spiritually, in short, in every arena of my life. I am a failure. It is not sufficient to be able to say these words; it is necessary to believe them in my heart. Scripturally, it's called humbling oneself.

This is not an esteem issue. It's not a victim mentality, where nothing is my fault. Everything is my fault, and I am the problem. Once I accept this, I become a useful tool for the kingdom. Until I do, my flesh is in the way. My pride wants the recognition. My spiritual power is weak. When being somebody important doesn't matter any longer, then I can enjoy life. I can accept the love and forgiveness Jesus offers. Until then, I cannot accept it, because I must measure up. I can't measure up. I must know and believe I can't measure up. This secret is opposite of much if not most of what is preached.

I know a tremendous preacher. His sermons have great insight, are well put together, and touch everyone. He is compassionate. It seems he hears from God. Yet there is a punch missing. This punch is serious spiritual power. I believe he studies long and prays hard. Unfortunately, I do not believe he has been broken. His strength, tremendous as it is, is a barrier to the serious power God has for him. He does not have a desperation in his heart to depend on God. He has not been humbled.

We can say the same things about prayer. We know people with punch in their prayers who get answers and others whose prayers are little more than a formality. Again, the difference is spiritual power.

There are many traps. We can have a form but not the real power of the Holy Spirit. We deceive ourselves by looking at the wrong things and comparing ourselves to others or false standards. We think manifestations of power are really the power, when they are only the symptom. We nurture our pride and ego. We insulate ourselves from the Holy Spirit breaking us. We listen to what others say about us. We have too high an opinion of ourselves, and it becomes all about us. In short, our sinful nature will do anything, and the devil will help it, to keep us from really humbling ourselves and gaining this power.

If I have this power, what will I do with it? The first purpose of serious spiritual power is to change my heart. The second is to strip away the deception of the devil, the world, and our flesh. The third is fulfilling our destiny in God, or saying it more clearly, to do what God created us to do.

Jesus said we would do greater things than He did (see John 14:12). What could that possibly be? Jesus raised the dead, walked on water, cast out demons, healed the sick, turned water into wine, and fed thousands. He blessed the downtrodden, cried with those that mourn, and in short, He did it all.

Yet scripture says, "I will strike the shepherd and the sheep will be scattered." (see Matthew 26:31). Of all the thousands He preached to, only John stood by the cross. Cephas, commonly believed to be Peter, walked to Emmaus and did not believe. Jesus had to explain how the scriptures predicted the resurrection—and this is after Cephas saw the empty tomb!

Jesus changed only a few hearts. After the ascension, as He promised, He sent the Comforter. In Luke 24:49, He says to "tarry in Jerusalem, until you are endued with Power from on High." This is an interesting choice of words. The power clearly comes from the Holy Spirit. As the apostles went about their business, they "turned the world upside down." Revelation says they overcame by the power of the word and their testimony (Revelations 12:11).

Today, most of the American church is a complacent, emasculated shell of what God wants. In area after area, we are little different from the world. God is calling us, with increasing urgency, to accept the offered spiritual power. Every day we make numerous decisions, decisions on who we are, what we do, what we think of, priorities, etc., that will either lead us toward increasing spiritual power or decreasing spiritual power. Let us be sure to make the right decisions. For the record, the call is to individuals, not an organization. God changing individuals will ultimately change the organization, but it rarely works the other way.

Much has been written and more said about changing hearts. Changing my heart is more than not doing sin, or replacing sin with righteousness. It includes the "being" things, the things so foreign to us that we have trouble describing them. It is not enough to do kind things, but we also must be fundamentally kind. The spiritual power to change us to be kind can only come from God. Jesus said in Matthew 15:19, "For out of the heart proceed evil thoughts, murders, adulteries, fornications, thefts, false witness, blasphemies. These are thing things that defile a man."

God really, really hates hypocrisy. Matthew 15:7–9 says, "Hypocrites! Well did Isaiah prophesy about you, saying 'These people draw near to Me with their mouth, and honor Me with their lips, but their heart is far from Me. And in vain they worship me, teaching as doctrine the commandments of men.'"

This is a sobering thought, for all of us have hearts different from what we want others to see. Mine frightens me, which is one reason I need serious spiritual power. My heart needs changing. Spiritual power is what changes my personal heart.

God requires purity to give power. He requires pure thoughts, desires, motives, and actions. Purity is the same as holiness. It is becoming set apart from the world's way to God's way. It is being consistent, even when no one is looking. It is being the same on the inside as it is on the outside. Our attitudes are not shaped by the world or circumstances but by God Himself. He has commanded us to be pure and holy as He is holy. Guile has no place in a pure person. We strive for purity, not so we can claim purity but because only the pure are worthy for the Ruler of eternity. Purity leads to power, which leads to more effectiveness for the kingdom of God.

It should be noted believers are given a robe of righteousness. This robe is the righteousness of Jesus covering our sins. We will always have sin, which is why we need that robe. This robe is our absolute purity. It cost Jesus everything, more than we can possibly understand. We should still strive for purity, not so we don't need the robe but because we love Jesus so much we want to emulate Him. In fact, not wanting to emulate Jesus (or saying it differently, love Him) is a clear warning about your spiritual status.

I want my words to have punch. I want to speak with the authority Jesus spoke with. He had the type of power I am talking about, and most people did not accept his words. But even His enemies wondered where He got His authority from. When you speak for God, with God's words, people are either drawn to Jesus or repulsed from you.

Complacency, the attitude "this is not my fight," is a major deception. When I get to eternity, I don't want to find out life was far more important than Friday night football, church on Sunday, or working hard in my job. These things are important, perhaps critical, but they are only a shadow of the truly important. We should have the attitude that at any moment, at any time, in any circumstance, God might call on us to speak to someone, if only an encouraging word, perhaps a smile. Or perhaps, when no one is looking, we should pick up trash in the bathroom. Maybe He only wants to touch our minds, make us aware of Him, perhaps a short prayer or instruction. I like to say I have my antennae up at all times, listening for the gentle, small, still, quiet voice of God, whispering secrets. It is not my job to understand how these things advance the kingdom. These things are a witness to Jesus. If it pleases God, the kingdom is advanced.

The first tool to discuss is intimacy. There are few things

I will not interrupt to take a phone call from my wife. She is special to me. I can share not just thoughts but experiences with her. The high points of my life are when we do things together, watch a movie, go to a restaurant, whatever. Intimacy means as much as possible she is part of my life—the outside, but especially the inside. I must be open and vulnerable, able to share my fears and hopes.

This is a good earthly example of God. He desires intimacy that goes far beyond that of people. He wants to know us, and for us to know Him. He wants us to know Him as God, but also as man, as the King of everything, but also as a friend. He wants us to understand His love, His concerns, and His plans. Intimacy goes way beyond these things, to a depth that cannot be described. I doubt that, while alive, any human, except perhaps Adam and Eve, has ever experienced the kind of intimacy God desires.

God wants us to tell Him our concerns. I know He might not act like I want, but I do know He wants me to talk to him. Several of my friends have "dumped" on me. I am not sure how I got this honor, but they let it all hang out. They know I will not think less of them for their sharing their struggles, their fears, their hopes, and their dreams. For sure I can't do anything. But a friend listens and cares, and they sense this. It is the same with God.

Knowledge is critical. Knowledge is a close relative to intimacy, but a little different. We need to be marinated in the facts of scripture. A bug should taste Bible verses when it bites us (a silly example). We can't do what the Bible says without knowing what the Bible says. Knowing Jesus the Christ gives us a little spiritual power. Knowing Him and His word increases our spiritual power far beyond our imagination.

Purity is important. Purity is more than what we do, but it is what we think and what we are—purity in thoughts, motives, actions, and most important desires. I have an enemy—actually several enemies. One of God's great acts of kindness, right up there with providing rain for our crops, is that He has not given me a quiver of lightning bolts. I say I want to only singe their eyebrows, but in truth, I want to miss the eyebrows and zap them between the eyes. I'm not really pure. My desire is for revenge. It hampers my spiritual power.

Purity goes far beyond this. Scripture talks about taking every thought captive. I believe everything includes our emotions as well. What are they captive to? They are captive to the person Jesus wants me to be and the direction of the Holy Spirit.

He is patient. Captivity says I should be patient. It is so hard, especially when some jerk keeps running his mouth. Or whatever.

Surrender, which is giving God control of our actions, thoughts, words, deeds, desires, and future, is important to spiritual power. The issue comes down to rebellion. Our rebellion is against God, as the ultimate King. Jesus conquered death, a great spiritual victory, but He clearly stated in the garden right before the cross "not my will but Your will" as He talked with the Father (see Matt. 26:39). Jesus said He did nothing unless He first heard if from the Father (see. He is our model, our example. There was no rebellion in Him. There should not be rebellion in us either. There can't be as we become more like the Christ.

We can do nothing for God except it is done in faith (see Hebrews 11:6). In Hebrews 11:1, God tells us faith is the evidence of things not seen and the substance of things hoped for. Another translation uses the word *conviction* instead of substance. I find it interesting that these are legal terms; evidence leads to a conviction. A judge friend assured me a judge cannot convict himself. It takes evidence to do this. I can't be convicted if I sign a confession, unless there is supporting evidence. The evidence is critical to the conviction. Convictions do not happen until the judge signs a paper (I believe it is called an "order"). His signature is his seal. Once he seals the order, the defendant is changed from a free person to a felon.

The Holy Spirit is our guarantee or seal (see 2 Corinthians 1:22). We have been sealed. Once sealed, we are changed from faithless to faithful. Just as I depend on my faithful dog, God depends on His faithful servants.

Incidentally, the greater the evidence, the greater the conviction. If arrested for speeding, I'm convicted of a misdemeanor; if assault, a felony; but if murder, I can be (in some states) executed.

Numerous times we are exhorted to believe. My opinion is that we decide to believe, but God then responds by giving us faith. We confuse these two, but they are different. Our beliefs cover many things, from how we should comb our hair, our political affiliations, what we will grow up to do, chocolate or vanilla ice cream, the Easter bunny, etc. Most of these are trivial but a matter of daily life. I believe my wife will get home from work at the normal time, but in fact, she may work overtime. Beliefs are our picture of reality.

Faith is the power to please God. This is in our obedience, our attitudes, our thoughts, and our desires. It is similar to the pipeline feeding a powerhouse. Big powerhouses take bigger pipelines. Faith is much bigger than simply believing.

In Romans 12:6, Paul talks about prophesying in measure of our faith. Big spiritual jobs require big faith.

Another key is direction. Jesus said He did nothing without first hearing from the Father. Paul talks about being guided by the Spirit. Little kids don't know how to talk, so they practice. When they grow up, they have learned speaking skills, and now we have many great orators. Godly direction is critical for true spiritual power. Acts 19:13–17 talks about how seven sons of Sceva tried casting a demon out by the name of Jesus, but without the direction of God. The demon responded by saying, "Jesus I know, and Paul I know, but who are you?"

Jesus talks about the hireling shepherd. Without the direction of God, we are little more than a hireling, a pretender. Who are we to determine these things? Only God should direct us, but we are often directed by ourselves.

How many times have I felt nudged by the Holy Spirit to go somewhere or do something? Sometimes it surely seems like the end result advances the kingdom, but other times, I have no idea. The bigger question is obedience to the direction of God.

The last tool is love. There is a lot written in scripture about love. When asked what was the greatest commandment, Jesus answered, "Love the Lord your God with all your heart, mind, and strength" (Matthew 22:37). He also said to love your neighbor as yourself. Then in the upper room, right before His crucifixion, He added another commandment, to love the brethren as He has loved us. Each of these are a decision, and in reality, they all flow from the first one. If I love God, I will love the things He loves.

The description of love is similar to addiction, the most powerful addiction possible. The truly addicted will sacrifice anything and everything for their addiction. The difference is love brings spiritual life while all other addictions bring death and bondage. Jesus said He came that we might have life and have it abundantly (see John 10:10).

We briefly discussed seven more tools for spiritual power—power that breaks deception, frustrating the devil's lies and his attempts to steal, to destroy, and to kill. Tools bringing life, advancing the kingdom, and pleasing God.

There are many other tools. Second Peter 1 adds virtue, self-control, perseverance, godliness, and brotherly kindness. There are other lists elsewhere. But one can achieve greater spiritual power by starting with these seven and adding the others as one studies scriptures and prays.

Let me repeat the seven tools: intimacy, knowledge, purity, surrender (of control), faith, devotion, and love.

In every case, we pay a price. It is no longer about us but about God. Something in us needs to be destroyed, whether it is our pride, our presumption, our time, or whatever. But God created us to replace our focus on ourselves but on the things of God. Our first, and most important, battle is in ourselves. It is the one place where we have total control over free will. We can choose the things of God or not. There is no resurrection without a crucifixion. Taking and applying these seven tools requires first putting our flesh to death and allowing God to resurrect them in our life.

We use spiritual power to clearly and consistently present Jesus, and Him crucified. Jude said in Jude 1:23, "We pull the lost from the fires, with their garments stained with smoke." Angels rejoice in heaven for every sinner turning to God (see Luke 15:10), and I believe we will join them when we get there. It will be one mind-blowing, awesome party.

A lie of the devil is it is not worth the price. Jim Elliot, a missionary who died trying to reach a South American tribe, said "He is no fool that gives up what he cannot keep to gain what he cannot lose." Jesus said, "If you are faithful in the small things, you will be given great things."

I went to a church lady's funeral. She was the ideal woman, good mother, and good citizen. She attended every church service, gave generously, constantly read her Bible, and prayed. In short, every preacher wants a church full of people like her. As I walked into the funeral home, God gave me a glimpse of where she was. I did not expect what I saw. In that instant, the vision I saw was of a physical darkness. I cannot describe the aloneness, emptiness, and isolation. But the worst of all was the fear, a tangible, smothering fear, suffocating the soul with a horror defying description. Going insane is not an option. The victim is fully aware in a perfect sense of everything.

This is the price of a lack of spiritual power. Perhaps you believe God is not for you. He has given you the right to make that decision. But make that decision clearly, consciously, without confusion. Spiritual power takes away the deception and lies, which conspire to confuse the issue. It provides the actions, whether it be speech, kindness, healing someone, to push the kingdom into lives where it would not otherwise be.

We will be held accountable in eternity for what we are in

this life. If we pursue spiritual power, true spiritual power, such that God can flow through us to do what He wants to do, then we will get "credit." This credit is not earning our salvation, but the rewards Paul talks of in 1 Corinthians 3:12–15. The gold and silver will pass through the fire of judgment, but the wood and straw will burn up. The foundation is Jesus the Christ. A foundation in Jesus will have great spiritual power.

I am rather greedy. I want to be rich. But I know I must invest to make money. I invested in college to get a good job. I bought property for appreciation, and it has returned nicely. Stocks and bonds all take giving up current money for more money later. Serious eternal wealth requires giving up puny "wealth" (which is more than money but our time, energy, and attitudes—in short, everything we are) today. Spiritual power, gained by submitting to God's plan, leads to great wealth in eternity.

From a human standpoint, we don't see the value of eternal riches. But our lives, which are now so big to us, are but a faint shadow of fog when compared to eternity.

The biggest prize and the most return of all is to hear Jesus say, "Well done, my good and faithful servant."

What about you? What do you want? Have you ever laid the foundation? Do you know Jesus? Are you pursuing purity? Do you want the spiritual power I discussed? How much power do you want? How comfortable are you? Is it for you? Beg God to direct us.

10

See the Times

My first ambition wants to sense God's presence on a continual basis. I want to be so filled with God's love that I have no room for selfish love. I want to hear the gentle wind of God's voice. I have a great desire to inspire others to have as much fruit in eternity as possible, which starts accumulating with their salvation but then continues to the rest of their life. Inner spiritual peace, which is different from other kinds of peace, is something I strive for. I do not naturally have boldness, yet I want to be bold for following Jesus. I believe it is ineffectual to try to be used of God without the power of God. Now I want to address my last ambition, which is to "see the times."

A friend of mine asked what "seeing the times" meant. In its simplest term, it is discernment or understanding the time period or season we are in. In more accurate terms, it discerns the dispensation or giving of God's grace for the now. Some theologians have stated there are seven dispensations of God's grace throughout history. A dispensation is a particular method that God uses to dispense His grace. For example, the

Mosaic law is one dispensation, which was replaced by grace at the cross and resurrection.

The seeing the times I am referring to is not referring to the big picture stuff given in scripture, regardless of whether there are three, seven, or ten dispensations. Instead, it is the more mundane, specific dispensation for a specific group. It is seeing what is going on right now.

Since my conversion, I have had several different dispensations of grace. Initially was a time when I learned everything I could about life with Jesus. I made many mistakes. Then I went on to a quiet service. I did a few things for God, like teach Sunday school, but mostly I grew, while I accumulated life experiences to later draw on. My mind was active, always thinking but especially thinking of the things of God. Then I began preaching, first in the county jail, and later in state prison. I miraculously understood many spiritual things and saw spiritual truths. In 2015, I moved into a new season, which is not yet entirely clear to me. It is always scary to change seasons, since we don't know what is ahead. It comes down to a loss of control. Since the season is new, I can't control it. I must let Jesus control it.

I used to be an engineer. Then the time to retire came, not because I could not do the work but because it was time. The season changed from being an engineer to a retired person. In this new season, I started helping nonprofits, which I could never have done when I was an engineer. I still have a lot of questions about this new season and am exploring my new role in God's kingdom. It could change again.

Each season has its own rules. In our natural world, a season including young children means we do things differently than in a season with only grown-up children. It is the same with spiritual seasons. Each has their own rules. Some rules apply to all seasons. There are a few rules specific to one season. The rules determine our roles.

It is important to see the season we are in. Our tendency is continuing doing the things we are comfortable with. But as scripture says in 2 Corinthians 5:17 (NKJV) "Therefore, if anyone *is* in Christ, *he is* a new creation; old things have passed away; behold, all things have become new."

This is as true for the different seasons as it is for us as a new creation compared to an old and natural man.

Every season has preparation. In my life, the preparation for successive seasons overlapped into the previous season. Moving from one season to another requires a massive change. Change is not easy for us humans. We struggle with it, we become comfortable with the previous season, and we don't want to change. To not embrace the changing of the seasons is to reject God's grace for us at this time, and in effect, rejecting God Himself. We must take full advantage of preparation times to be effective in our new seasons.

I enjoyed my first season. God was so close, and it seemed like He continually directed me. But the time came when it was necessary for me to leave the cocoon He made for me and enter the cold, cruel world. He had work for me, and I needed to be about it. The change was difficult, and I wanted to go back many times.

Jesus went through different times or seasons. Up until He was about twelve, He was subject to his mother. At age twelve scripture says He grew in favor with God and man. Several years later, starting with the wedding in Canaan, He went through several seasons; some writers divide them into His public and private ministry. He had a season of sacrifice, culminating with the cross. Then He had a forty-day season of ministry to His followers, which culminated in the ascension. Now He is in a season making intercession for us at the right hand of the Father.

Seeing the times is a critical skill, and the secular world pays big bucks for people who can do this. Every brokerage firm has experts who look at everything they can, building all kinds of mathematical models, to see the times and better choose higher-preforming stocks versus those that do not do well. Governments hire all kinds of people to "see the times" for world events, their economies, and crop forecasts.

Spiritually, God has occasionally gifted certain people with a special ability to see the seasons or times. We see this in 1 Chronicles 12:32 (NKJV): "Of the sons of Issachar who had understanding of the times, to know what Israel ought to do."

Knowing the times is different from a prophet, although the two ministries often overlap. Jeramiah saw the season regarding Babylon's conquest of Judah, and he was also a prophet. The prophet speaks for God, while one who knows the times understands the day and age he or she is in.

> Scripture talks abundantly about the different seasons. To everything *there is* a season, A time for every purpose under heaven: A time to be born, And a time to die; A time to plant, And a time to pluck *what is* planted; A time to kill, And a time to heal; A time to break down, And a time to build up; A time to weep, And a time to

laugh; A time to mourn, And a time to dance; A time to cast away stones, And a time to gather stones; A time to embrace, And a time to refrain from embracing; A time to gain, And a time to lose; A time to keep, And a time to throw away; A time to tear, And a time to sew; A time to keep silence, And a time to speak; A time to love, And a time to hate; A time of war, And a time of peace. (Ecclesiastes 3:1–8 NKJV)

Daniel saw the season had changed and began praying for his people to return to Judah. He knew the season of captivity had ended. Point of interest: sometimes it takes a discerning person to "pray in" the new season.

In the New Testament, Matthew 16:2–3 (NKJV) says, "He (Jesus) answered and said to them, 'When it is evening you say, "*It will be* fair weather, for the sky is red"; and in the morning, "*It will be* foul weather today, for the sky is red and threatening." Hypocrites! You know how to discern the face of the sky, but you cannot *discern* the signs of the times.'"

Jesus orders us to understand the seasons. He is talking not about weather but about the spiritual seasons we are in.

I am using seasons interchangeably with times. We understand the word *seasons* better than the word *times*, although in the context I'm using, they are the same thing.

Jesus himself came at the perfect time, a special season.

Galatians 4:4 (NKJV) says, "But when the fullness of the time had come, God sent forth His Son, born of a woman, born under the law."

The concept is time was "pregnant" with anticipation for

Jesus. It was the perfect timing for Him to come. Today we look back and can list many of the things that make it the right time. The Romans conquered most of Europe, the Middle East, and northern Africa. The Roman peace marked their rule. They built roads all over their empire, making travel easier.

Before the Romans, the Greeks conquered much of the same world and spread the Greek language. Not only was travel easier, but there was also a common language (at least among the educated), making the spread of the gospel easier. And so it goes.

Our human season is different from God's.

John 7:6 (NKJV) says, "Then Jesus said to them, "My time has not yet come, but your time is always ready."

In other words, God's season is perfect. We, as people, can sometimes naturally see seasons, but they might not be the same as God's season. We are impatient, eager to see the outcome. Jesus is patient, willing to nurture the situation to make it perfect.

I see so many people either ahead of or behind God. They sense there is a specific season, but they either move too soon or procrastinate.

God commanded King Saul to wait until Samuel came and offered the sacrifice. Saul moved ahead of God and was severely punished for his disobedience. He could not wait for the right season, and as a result, he lost his kingdom (see 1 Samuel 15:1–11).

It is not enough to know the seasons or the times. It is critical to see the spiritual season and see it, not through human eyes, but through godly eyes.

God has appointed a season for everything, and I want to

know what that season entails. On a personal level, I want to know how to act. I am between seasons right now. The real question is how I will use my time to the best preparation. Knowing the seasons will help me.

Churches can be between seasons. One pastor leaves, and a new one comes. It is the same with business. Bosses come and go. Our country is in a different season than it was a few years ago. What are the new rules? Few people know.

There is a season for spiritual harvest. Jesus said in John 4:35 (NKJV), "Do you not say, 'There are still four months and *then* comes the harvest'? Behold, I say to you, lift up your eyes and look at the fields, for they are already white for harvest!" By the way, the term *white* refers to the color change a grain makes when it becomes ripe.

All around us are souls hungry for the love and peace and purpose only Jesus can provide. People look for direction; they want to know what to do. We must be about the harvest. The question is always, "How?"

Jesus marked a changing of the seasons when He died for our sins on a painful cross. Harvest time is now here.

Everyone needs to know what season he or she is in. My ambition is to understand the season of my church, my community, and those organizations I'm a part of. One organization is very effective in reaching the lost. We went from a prosperous time to a time when members left, our work went undone, morale was low, and we wondered if we should continue. The group took my suggestion to change how we prayed. Nothing changed, and we barely eked by. Until, little by little, we began rebuilding.

The gap was a passing of the baton to the next generation.

God wanted us to prepare for that change. When it came, we needed to do things differently. The new people had uncomfortable ideas. Some were outside our charter. Yet, we did not dismiss them but worked to determine if there was a modification to bring their idea into our mission. We started moving them into leadership roles, with the explanation that these were steps to greater leadership.

The point is, I understood the changing of the seasons, and the organization used their time between seasons to prepare. The same principles (seasons change and there are times of preparation) apply to individuals.

What season are you in? Is it about to change? What are the new rules for a changed season? Are you in a time of preparation? Don't let it be an excuse, because even in preparation times, God has things for you to do.

Everyone is either in a season or between seasons. If you don't know what your season is, then ask God. I believe He wants His people to know what season they are individually in.

We can always prepare for whatever season we are in by reading the Bible, prayer, etc. Spiritual disciplines are always appropriate. (An excellent reference is *Celebration of Discipline* by Richard J. Foster, published by Harper and Row.)

Maybe you think you have blown it, gone too far, done too much, or are too bad. God's grace is sufficient to forgive everyone. If He forgave me, He can forgive you. If He can use me, He can use you. Our job is to find out what we are to do in this new season.

Now could be a change of seasons for you. Perhaps if you have never made Jesus your life's boss, you could change seasons. Maybe you think you are in a dry season when, although you have Jesus as your savior, He seems far away, like He forgot you. He has not forgotten you. He wants all of us to be in a season of spiritual plenty, where we are doing what He wants us to do. Our rewards are not in this life but in the next, and that life is a lot longer.

You are in a change of seasons if you are refining and defining your spiritual ambitions.

11

Setting Your Spiritual Ambitions, Part II

How should one go about determining spiritual ambitions? We talked about this in chapter 2. To briefly review several key steps:

1. relationship with God
2. honesty
3. hearing from God (are your ambitions the same as His for you?)
4. willingness to implement the ambitions you hear from God
5. researching each one in scripture.

Everything starts with a relationship with God. Without a relationship, the end is at best futility, and at worst, hell. Base your spiritual ambitions on first starting and then building a relationship with Jesus.

Romans 10:9–10 (NKJV) tells us, "That if you confess with

your mouth the Lord Jesus and believe in your heart that God has raised Him from the dead, you will be saved. For with the heart one believes unto righteousness, and with the mouth confession is made unto salvation." You can't confess a lie. If you confess Jesus is Lord, then for it to be a confession, He must be your Lord. Lord means your source of everything, from daily direction to where we find satisfaction. Justification before God is a heart type of belief, not intellectual (although the intellect is involved).

Once you have a basic relationship, the next step is deepening and growing the relationship. I love Jesus both differently and more than I did when I first believed.

Honesty is critical. It is necessary to brutally examine one's motives, desires, and thoughts. A bad ambition is one you want to have because of wrong motives. Your ambitions are tainted if your desire is to be well-liked. This is difficult, and most of us are unable to sort through these conflicts without specific help from the Holy Spirit. Ask for it. Contaminated ambitions result in a contaminated person who has no eternal fruit.

A major step is what the apostle Paul said: "To put to death the deeds of the body" (Romans 8:13 NKJV). The deeds of the body include human desires. I personally like attention. Yet I must consider my human desire as if it were dead. To do this, I carefully look for ways to minister that others don't see. What I want is automatically suspect. This is why honesty is so important. We are experts at tricking ourselves. Only with the Holy Spirit's help (who Jesus called the Spirit of Truth John 14:17) can we be truly honest.

I suggest you consider ambitions in these categories:

1. Relationship to God
2. The kind of Christian you will be
3. How you will serve.

I believe my first three are almost universally desired by God for His people.

They are:

- to feel God's presence
- to be filled with God's love
- to sense the gentle wind of God

You'll want the spiritual ambitions Jesus wants you to have if you really have made Jesus Lord. This means you must hear from God, which requires prayer (and possibly fasting). Part of prayer is listening. When I developed my list, the first several came easily. I knew there were more, but it became harder to listen. It took me almost two weeks for me to identify "seeing the times" as an ambition. God may have been speaking all along, but I surely didn't hear. I knew there was more because I felt the list was incomplete. Hearing takes patience. I felt a sense of completeness from the Holy Spirit after including the last ambition.

I can't emphasize this next point enough. It is important to have already decided to implement the list before you start. God is not interested in conditional obedience, where we hear His will and then decide if we will follow Him. We need to decide up front that we will obey and quickly obey. You must follow through once you complete your list. It is no good to have a list only to ignore it.

Finally, it is important to research each of your ambitions

in scripture. I spent about two weeks developing each of my ambitions. I thought about them as I drove to work, at home, and in any free time. I thought about relevant scriptures. I made notes and then organized these notes. Only research from scripture counts. It doesn't matter what your pastor or favorite author says, unless it points to scripture.

Some of my research surprised me. I found, as God guided my research, that seeing the times is much different than I initially expected. I believe it's God's plan for me, yet when I made my initial list, my concept was totally different than after I completed my study.

I have the advantage of having read the Bible multiple times, which meant the Holy Spirit could bring verses to my mind. Perhaps one of your ambitions it to become familiar with scripture.

If I had done this as a new believer, I would have come up with a totally different list, with more shallow research. That's okay. It is reasonable that one's ambitions change as life happens. It did in my secular career. If I live long enough, it is likely my spiritual ambitions will mature more.

God created you for a purpose, like everyone else. Determining God's ambitions for you, and then focusing your life in that direction, will help keep you from getting sidetracked. You will have the life that pleases God as much as possible. You will have the maximum possible amount of fruit in eternity.

Remember, your ambitions define you, which determine what you do, resulting in either good or bad fruit for eternity. Choose wisely.

Go for it!

Printed in the United States
By Bookmasters